CREATING
Pantomime

CREATING
Pantomime

JOYCE BRANAGH AND KEITH ORTON

THE CROWOOD PRESS

First published in 2011 by
The Crowood Press Ltd
Ramsbury, Marlborough
Wiltshire SN8 2HR

www.crowood.com

British Library Cataloguing-in-Publication Data
A catalogue record for this book is available from the British Library.

ISBN 978 1 84797 255 2

Front cover: Jack and the Beanstalk, with Ricardo Coke-Thomas as Jack (talking beanstalk voiced by Alice Jackson, made by Mike Bell and June Douglas).
Back cover: Howard Coggins as Sarah the Cook in the underwater scene from Dick Whittington and his Cat (costume by John Brooking, lighting design by John Harris).
Frontispiece: The 'dancing' Daisy the Cow and Silly Billy in Jack and the Beanstalk (Alice Jackson and Martine Burt as Daisy, with Dale Superville as Silly Billy, choreography by Nikki Woollaston).

The photographs that accompany each chapter feature pantomime productions at Watford Palace Theatre and were taken by Keith Orton unless otherwise stated.

Typeset by Sharon Kemmett, Isis Design.
Printed and bound in Singapore by Craft Print International

CONTENTS

INTRODUCTION

A PASSION FOR CREATING PANTOMIME

The Yuletide pantomime is the biggest show of the year for most theatres. Taking the most time to produce (so many sets and costumes), it makes the most money (helping sustain a theatre through more difficult times) and gets the most 'bums on seats', making it the production that reaches the most people in the local community. For many people, the annual pantomime is the only time they will go to a theatre all year – it's a family event, bringing generations together. For many young children a pantomime is their first experience of theatre – ever. So for all these reasons, it's important to get it right!

What we are describing in this book is by no means the definitive method of creating a pantomime. If all the experts and pantomime aficionados were gathered in one room and given the task of defining what makes for the best pantomime, they would all come to a different conclusion. So what we intend to do is explain what we have learned and offer up our own particular practice as a guide to those who might be approaching it for the first time, or want to review what they are already doing.

The synthesis of writing and design

One of the main reasons for writing this book is to share a passion for pantomime that has grown over the past five years of our collaboration. What we mean by 'creating' is starting with the idea of staging a pantomime and developing the script and the design alongside each other from the very beginning. This method of working can be creatively rewarding, but is not always possible due to time, budget or existing production processes in theatres. However, it is worth striving for because when this collaboration is successful, it is often difficult to see any separation, particularly with the humour and the styling. It is when this synthesis between writer/director and designer exists that we believe the most successful pantomime is created.

What we suggest is by no means the usual process. Pantomimes are less likely to be created in this inclusive way. Most design is done once a script has at least got to first draft. What we are demonstrating here is a process where the writer/director and designer can discuss and exchange ideas before either of them undertakes their own particular specialist role. After all, the writing and design together create the storytelling, and with audiences seeing the final pantomime as

OPPOSITE: *Peter Holdway as Fleshcreep in* Jack and the Beanstalk *(lighting design by John Harris).*

7

a whole, it is so much better when the humour and spectacle flow as one.

The joy of developing initial ideas in a creative team is that there is always someone there to bounce ideas off. Some of Britain's most successful comedy writers have been double acts for this very reason. It is so important that the writer and the designer appreciate each other's talents and can know when to let the other take the lead. As a partnership, writer and designer can at times be a struggle, but it is through this struggle and understanding of each other's strengths in storytelling that a successful outcome is achieved.

For the designer it enables them to be truly involved in the development of the narrative and have the visual lead in some of that development. For a writer it gives them the opportunity to test out the narrative visually within the writing process rather than hope that what they have written can be recreated and played out on stage. Alongside this, the designer's view of their role in theatre is changing: quite a lot are choosing to view themselves as scenographers (that is, looking beyond purely designing the sets and costumes, to a more complete involvement in the creation of performance).

In recent years there has been a growing interest, both regionally and commercially, in creating new productions, creating more opportunities for this type of collaboration. Although we will concentrate on this inclusive method of working, most of the processes and techniques that we describe are easily transferable to other ways of creating pantomime.

Resurgence of pantomime

Commercial and regional pantomime have had a resurgence in recent years with major actors and writers engaging with, and aiding in, the rebirth of the traditions and quality of pantomime. The likes of Sir Ian McKellen and Simon Callow, and writers, Stephen Fry, Mark Ravenhill and Jonathan Harvey have got themselves involved in these new pantomime productions, and together with theatres such as the Barbican, the Old Vic and the Hackney Empire, have all contributed to raising its profile and brought traditional pantomime back to the Capital. Within commercial pantomimes, production companies such as Qdos Entertainment and First Family Entertainment have invested heavily in creating new pantomime productions with high production values, which will be touring the major regional theatres for several years to come.

This increase in interest has meant that the genre has gained a higher importance and also has prompted theatres up and down the country to take greater care and pride in the quality of the pantomimes that they are producing. This, combined with the growth in theatre technologies, has given pantomime the opportunity to review its style and composition for the twenty-first century.

Raising the bar

Just because it is an annual event, with an almost guaranteed box office, pantomime should not be taken for granted – if standards slip then so will the audiences. If a pantomime does not live up to people's expectations and memories, or it is too non-traditional, then audiences will probably choose to go elsewhere next year. After all there are hundreds up and down the country to choose from. We want to banish the phrase, 'Oh that will do, it is only panto.'

Pantomime entails months of preparation with long hours of writing and designing to get it right, but should never lose the element of fun along the way. If the sense of fun is lost then pantomime can become a chore. It is with a strong sense of purpose, and serious amounts of time spent in the development of the script and design, where the quality of the final show shines through. You can have the best performers in the world, but if they have a poor script and ineffectual costumes and scenery then their performance will inevitably feel unsupported.

When speaking to anyone that has grown up being taken to the pantomime in their childhood, it is apparent that it is something that stays with them. The remembrance of the fun and spectacle is a strong memory and can be revitalized the minute the band strikes up and the lights dim. It is a British tradition that is unswervingly popular in good or bad economic times – there is always room for the annual trip to pantomime. The joy of pantomime is being able to leave the adult at the door to the theatre, and become that child again once in the auditorium. This is something that British audiences have been brought up on and may be one of the reasons why pantomime has endured.

Because of the nature of collaboration and the subject of pantomime, although the chapters in this book are laid out in chronological order, there are times when inevitably the subjects discussed delve into the whole process, or make reference to subjects discussed in other chapters. Some aspects will also be repeated for the sake of clarity when the reader uses this as a handbook.

This book might be read alongside *Pantomime* by Tina Bicât, also published by The Crowood Press. There will be examples and methodology that are only covered in one or the other, and viewpoints might differ, so reading both will give the reader a broader understanding. The primary difference is that this book concentrates on new writing and developing the script and design in tandem.

We'll be discussing and sharing our own ideas and experiences gained whilst writing, designing and directing pantomimes, primarily at Watford Palace Theatre, which has a long tradition for staging excellent pantomimes. This will be supported by examining the work, ideas, and experiences of other 'pantomime aficionados'. In this way, we hope to demonstrate what you need to consider, and what you need to do, to establish successful creative partnerships and productions. We hope that our passion for pantomime is infectious and that you will catch the bug and are enthused to go away and create the best pantomime you possibly can.

1. GETTING PREPARED

Before beginning the writing and design processes, there are several decisions that must be made to make sure that you understand for whom and why you have chosen to create the pantomime.

DO YOU HAVE THE RIGHT CREDENTIALS?

Creating a pantomime is a unique type of theatre production and will not suit all writers and designers. Without most of the attributes listed below you may struggle with its development. It can seem, on the surface, a superficial and straightforward task. After all, there is a formula to follow and this formula has been tried and tested for decades. But this can feel restricting to some and the fast pace of change and the sheer quantity of decisions to be made can be daunting. But if you have the skills and understand fully what you are undertaking then it can be a joyous experience.

As a writer ...

You need to be able to follow some of the 'rules' of pantomime story and structure, but also be able to use your imagination, to inject these old stories with new life. An endless supply of silly jokes is essential, and willingness to research and respect the genre is crucial. You need the knowledge of what children and their families are 'into', and knowing what makes them laugh is a distinct advantage. Pantomime writing deadlines are often strict and early, so an ability to get the outline, first draft, and final draft to the director, producer and designer on time is very important. Writing a pantomime requires an attitude that takes writing pantomime as seriously as any straight play, but also delights in getting a daft joke exactly right. Working at this you will be rewarded with happy faces, enormous laughs and excited squeals filling the auditorium night after night.

As a designer ...

It is important that you have strong illustrative skills. The genre requires a hand-drawn quality that is difficult to reproduce using computer-aided design techniques. You must have a good sense of humour and playfulness that you can bring to the way that you envisage and draft the scenery and costumes. You must be unafraid of colour and have a good knowledge of the materials (both costume and scenic materials), and a certain amount of mechanical understanding to enable you to tackle the tricky set pieces within the stories such as

OPPOSITE: *Christopher Robert as Dame Felicity Trott in* Jack and the Beanstalk *(costume made by Dawn Evans).*

11

flying carpets and beanstalks. Most importantly, to work with a writer, you must have a keen interest in how the visuals can progress the story.

As a director ...

You need to know about the traditions of pantomime, be able to cast the best available actors, singers and comedians, and bring a creative team together who work well and get the best from each other. You need to enjoy pantomimes, and bring that enjoyment to the production, thereby creating a show that is fast-paced, fun and frivolous, but which also captures the hearts of the audience.

Together ...

The creative team should relish creating something that they can take pride in but are not precious about. Time and money will dictate changes that are impossible to predict at the beginning of the process, and most importantly, the cast will bring along fresh ideas and personalities that will challenge the creative team's initial plans and the way that the script is delivered.

A creative team is most successful when they admire each other's work, but allow each person space to create in their own way. They should always take the production seriously but not themselves. Finally they must make each other laugh – it will help establish a more cohesive relationship and see you through the difficult moments that are bound to occur. If you can make each other laugh then there is a good chance the audiences will follow suit.

How long will it take to develop the script and design?

This will obviously depend upon the scale of the production, but consider beginning the writing and designing process a minimum of seven months prior to the opening. This is by no means full time throughout, but it does need that length of time to develop a well-conceived script and design and get it all realized to a good standard.

IS THERE AN AUDIENCE OUT THERE?

If your theatre, company or group has a tradition of producing pantomimes then you already know the answer to this question – though you will still need to do all you can to attract and keep your loyal audience. If pantomime is a relatively new venture, then you may want to consider a few things:

- What are the other theatres/companies/groups doing in your area? If there are a lot of pantomimes around, are you fighting for the same audience? If other pantomimes are on offer in your area, are they large commercial ones with big names, your local Repertory Theatre, smaller companies, or amateur productions? Basically, do you have competition within your size of production? If so, you may want to think about your choice of story, and how your production will differ. Will yours be more affordable/right on the doorstep/have a local celebrity, etc?

- What are the actual dates and times of your performances? By planning ahead, you can maximize your potential to attract an audience. Many companies now have performances (often two) on Sundays, and instead have Mondays off. If you can do day-time performances you may be able to attract a schools audience. If you start your production's run before a rival, then your review will be in the local papers earlier, and may attract more bookings. If you are doing a short run, then you might like to talk to other pantomime producers in the area and see if you can choose dates that don't clash. For instance, one company might opt for the week before Christmas and another the week after, both great choices for attracting those Yuletide audiences. Whatever you do, don't just think, 'Well, it's panto – of course people will come.' Do your research and you'll be in a much better position to achieve a successful sold-out run.

Who will your audience be?

Consider who the pantomime is for: what age group are they? This will influence the script-writing style, the choice of music, and the style of the sets and costumes.

Under-sevens

If your audience is going to be mostly children under the age of seven, then when writing the script, keep the language and story fairly simple, perhaps tailoring jokes to that age group. Small children like short jokes, which they can learn and repeat later! You should avoid loud bangs, darkness and baddies who are too sinister. They respond well to friendly characters with lots of interaction, and a good messy slosh scene (*see* Chapter 4) always goes down well!

With very young children lots of music can be a great idea, but keep pieces short or they will lose interest.

With sets and costumes, use children's book illustrations as a key style reference. The choice of colours and patterns will be bold with a strong use of primary colours. They also respond really well to whimsical elements within the sets, and enjoy looking for little details that have been designed into the backcloths and set pieces.

It is important that all these things combined hold a young audience's attention. You soon know when you have got it wrong: the audience gets fidgety and noisy.

Never underestimate what this age group will understand – making things too simple can lead to boredom. If you are unfamiliar with this age group a bit of research, such as watching young children's television, can give you an insight into

The milking scene from Jack and the Beanstalk. *The style and colours of the design were chosen with the younger-aged audience in mind (actors: Christopher Robert as Dame Felicity Trott; Dale Superville as Silly Billy; Alice Jackson and Martine Burt as Daisy the Cow).*

what might interest these young audience members.

Adults and over-eighteens

If it's a purely adult audience, or students over eighteen, then you may want to go more risqué with the script and jokes. There should be topical modern references that your audience will get – local characters, news headlines, politicians, celebrities, and so on. Rude jokes are essential, and depending on your audience, you may choose to include coarse language (though regular innuendo, double entendres and the threat of a swear word are often more effective than the real thing). The storyline matters less than writing a show that is good fun; however, you should keep the main plot elements for each story or the audience may feel cheated. You need to be clear in your advertising that this isn't for kids – for example, 'Sinderella...' – so that you don't have complaints at the end of the evening!

Here, the use of colour and materials will need a more adult approach. Suspenders, basques and suggestive props can heighten the raunchiness and risqué writing. Going this far with your concept will make it more difficult to stick to some of the traditions that exist within pantomime. However, it does allow for a more adult use of audience participation, similar to *The Rocky Horror Show* where the actors improvise and respond to direct heckling from the audience.

Specific groups

You may want to produce a pantomime for a specific audience who are a collective and who know each other personally. This might be the local sports club, school or college, local church, hobby society, workforce, or even prison. If so, think about what will work for them – are there any 'in' jokes, or songs or music associated with a particular group? For instance, if it was the Brownies you might want to make gentle jokes at Brown Owl's expense and include the club song.

Local themes and topical items of news can be portrayed through sets, costumes and props using such things as football shirts, local signs, business and street names; even the choice of pantomime characters could echo real-life people within a particular group.

Pantomime for a family audience

In most cases pantomimes are created for a family audience, aiming to be 'something for everyone', which can be harder than it sounds. With the script, keep the storyline fairly clear. Fill your design and script with silly jokes, combined with some topical references, but make sure these references aren't in any way lewd. Some pantomimes use a lot of innuendo in their jokes; this can work well, but if the jokes are too far above the kids' heads, then the adults miss the next section of the pantomime answering 'Why was that funny, Mummy?' over and over again.

Pace is incredibly important: if the pantomime has a slosh scene which the kids are enjoying, don't let it go on too long or the adults will become bored. Similarly a slow ballad, however well sung, will lose the interest of a seven-year-old pretty quickly, and then that child will get fidgety and ruin the parents' enjoyment. Keep the scenes/sections short, and then everyone will be happy.

As most pantomimes are directed at the family audience, and because this is the type of pantomime we have been creating over the past few years, we will concentrate on this type throughout the book. Just bear in mind that if catering for a different audience group you may need to modify your ideas to suit.

WHICH PANTOMIME STORY DO YOU CHOOSE?

There are numerous established stories to select from. Below is a list of the most popular and some useful tips that might help when deciding which story to choose. However, each story will require much more research into its origins, its traditional structure and plot, before making your final decision.

The fast-paced opening number led by Howard Coggins as Sarah the Cook in Dick Whittington and his Cat *(actors: Alice Jackson and Sia Kiwa; lighting design by John Harris).*

Traditional pantomimes

Cinderella

Perhaps the most coherent and best loved of all the pantomime stories, but can be an expensive pantomime to stage due to large set requirements and the need for two 'dames' (the Ugly Sisters, and therefore the associated costumes). The big challenge in *Cinderella* is the transformation scene. However, this is statistically the most popular show and excellent for box office sales, though it can seem more appealing to girls.

Aladdin

A great story that is well known to families, with a wonderful 'baddie'. The staging challenges could be the cave of wonders and the flying carpet (though not always present). Costumes are less fitted in style and as a result can be less expensive to make. Some of the basic costumes can be sourced more easily on the high street or websites. But, it can be costly when using pyrotechnics, due to the many appearances of the Genie and the Spirit of the Ring.

Dick Whittington and his Cat

This story demands more locations, which can be expensive. The big spectacle moment is the sinking of the ship, the *Saucy Sally*. The show needs enough of a chorus to provide the team of 'evil rats'. This is the only pantomime based on a real person.

Jack and the Beanstalk

A great fairytale, though less well known to modern children. The moral of the story can also be a little unclear. The interesting challenges here are how to stage the growth and climbing of the beanstalk and how to create the Giant. The story has a good 'animal friend' which is the family cow. This is a pantomime that appeals equally to boys and girls.

Something a bit different

The above are the 'top four' pantomimes in the UK, that is to say that theatre producers have found these titles produce the best ticket sales, year on year, particularly *Cinderella* and *Aladdin* as they have had popular films made, which most of the family are familiar with. So if attracting a large audience is crucial to you financially, you may want to bear this in mind. However, if your theatre already has a strong following, or you know that your audience wants something a bit different, there are other popular titles.

Snow White and the Seven Dwarfs

Being from a Grimm Brothers fairytale it has a good pantomime story with a strong heroine and handsome prince (who shows up late in the story). It has a really good baddie in the Wicked Queen, but its most interesting challenge is what to do about the seven dwarfs. It can be difficult to find suitable short adult actors and casting children is tricky as the roles can be quite demanding. Due to the rights to the film being with Disney, the dwarfs cannot have the film names 'Grumpy', 'Dopey', 'Doc', etc., so new names have to be invented.

Mother Goose

This is less well known as a story and it does not have the number of twists and recognizable magical moments that others have. As a spectacle, the dame has to transform in the Pool of Youth. Much more of a children's story, it may appeal less to the adults.

Babes in the Wood

This is rarely done today, which might be due in part to the abandonment of the children in the story. The story is often linked with the Robin Hood fable and its associated characters.

Puss in Boots

Again, this is not done often as the story has a theme close to Dick Whittington. Also, having the central character as a skin part/animal friend (actor dressed as Puss) makes it more difficult to cast this as a recognizable actor as their face may be too hidden as part of the costume.

Pantomimes based on children's books

The following pantomimes are based on classic children's books, have a strong association with Walt Disney films and/or the dame is either non-existent or plays a much reduced role in these stories, making it appear less traditional.

Beauty and the Beast

A great story and known by families through the Disney film. It seems to be getting more popular as a pantomime choice as it has the 'Cinderella appeal', and the potential for Ugly Sisters, but can be seen as a story mainly 'for girls'. Moments of magic will need to be considered in the design and costing.

Sleeping Beauty

This is a good story for pantomime with strong use of a prop (the spinning wheel) and another iconic baddie in the form of the wicked fairy. It also gives the option for more than one good fairy, which can create an interesting dynamic. The forest of thorns which grows and shields the castle for a hundred years can be a technical challenge. It is a story that does not have an obvious role for the dame.

Robinson Crusoe

A good story to have a principal boy as it is much more of an adventure. It will need additional writing (pre-story) before the shipwreck and when Robinson gets stranded on the desert island, to enable you to get the traditional pantomime characters into the story. It can also have quite a few parallels with *Dick Whittington*.

Peter Pan

This isn't technically a pantomime, but it is a very exciting story that everyone knows, and has in the past couple of years come out of copyright from the J.M. Barrie estate. On paper it is the most expensive to stage, due to the multiple locations of the Darlings' house and then all over the island in Neverland. It will require a large cast and its most technical challenge is how to do the flying of Peter and the Darling children. (When working professionally the flying must meet strict health and safety guidelines and may require outside professionals to facilitate this.) Even with amateur pantomimes it is really important that you are not endangering the actors by taking risks using unorthodox methods and equipment.

More unusual titles

The following are more unusual pantomimes that are seldom done but can be a good choice where you are in competition for some of the more popular titles.

Sinbad the Sailor, Goldilocks and the Three Bears, Little Red Riding Hood, Humpty Dumpty

All of these will need much adaptation and interpretation to make them into a pantomime story, but they can be a refreshing alternative to the more traditional versions that are seen repeatedly up and down the country. Little Red Riding Hood was one of the stories first selected for pantomime back in the nineteenth century.

If after all this you are still enthusiastic about putting on your own pantomime then the next chapter will help inform you of the important pantomime traditions that should be considered when contemplating your own version.

2 PANTOMIME TRADITIONS

Many shows are advertised as 'traditional family pantomimes'. By using the word 'family' the producer wants to indicate its suitability for a wide variety of ages (so if using this word in publicity material make sure that it is suitable for the whole family). The word 'traditional' can have further interpretations. It can mean that the pantomime is using an existing old script. It could also indicate that the producers have included traditional 'pantomime' elements such as a slosh scene, music, and perhaps a 'skin part' (animal character). Or it might suggest that the story is 'traditional' such as *Cinderella* or *Aladdin*. Or, less likely but not impossible, it might mean that they have completely adhered to the traditions of pantomime from the late nineteenth century. The audience understands tradition as 'familiarity', that there will be elements of the story, characters and setting that they recognize – perhaps from years of pantomime attendance.

Pantomime has been running to an established set of traditions that have preserved some, but not all, of the historical foundations that created this uniquely British form of theatre. Britain is credited with creating what we now know as pantomime from various other theatrical genres of the eighteenth and nineteenth centuries. The following is a very brief history. For a more thorough analysis, refer to the books listed in the Further Reading section at the back of this book.

HOW DID IT COME INTO BEING?

Its roots can be traced back to the theatrical form of commedia dell'arte, which was introduced from Italy, via Paris, to London and then British audiences where it became an immediate success. In its early development something called a Harlequinade was created. This saw traditional stories involving the commedia dell'arte characters (such as Harlequin, Columbine etc.) have other business such as magic, tricks, acrobatics, clowning and transformations added. It became a huge theatrical piece and within this Harlequinade the dialogue was secondary to the spectacle.

Eventually these early pantomimes were given titles and plots from popular fairytales and myths. Initially the shows were split into two distinct parts, there was an opening where the stories were told, followed by the huge spectacle of the Harlequinade. Then in the mid-nineteenth century, Drury Lane Theatre and the Lyceum Theatre (synonymous with the development of

OPPOSITE: *The slosh scene from* Dick Whittington and his Cat *(actors: Dale Superville and Howard Coggins).*

19

pantomime) began the process of expanding the opening so that the whole show became more narrative-driven and the Harlequinade began to fade out.

By the late 1800s Drury Lane Theatre was creating some of the most lavish and spectacularly staged pantomime productions, but alongside this, they began introducing comedians such as Dan Leno from the British Music Hall. These Music Hall stars no doubt added a higher profile and were in some ways brought in to increase the appeal and add to the box office takings by bringing their own fans with them. Such stars as Marie Lloyd, Little Titch, Herbert Campbell and especially Dan Leno, brought with them their own acts, cross-dressing and gags, and began to set several of the traits that have lasted right through to today.

It is interesting to note that when these Music Hall stars were introduced it created a similar uproar to the use of 'celebrities' in pantomime today. In each of its incarnations the public have always been unsure and at times vocal about changing a much-loved genre.

Honouring the past

It is important to have at least a basic understanding of how the modern pantomime came into being, before beginning to write and design your own. This is not suggesting the creation of historic replicas, but that any new ideas and twists on the retelling of the stories are introduced in the knowledge of why things were there in the first place. New and interesting approaches can be very exciting for the creative team and the audiences, but it is always necessary to question how this might be changing a

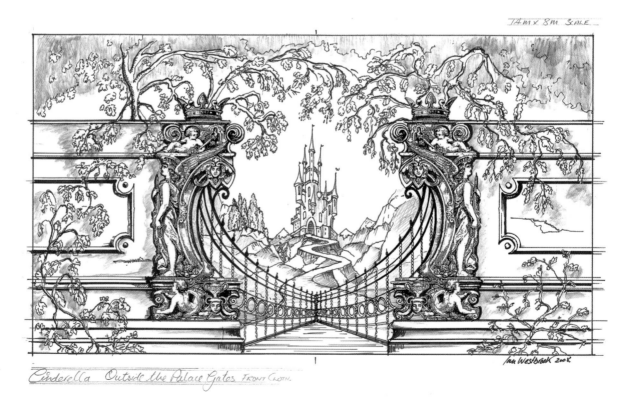

The Palace gates from Cinderella, *showing a storybook palace that is instantly recognizable as traditional (design by Ian Westbrook).*

production into something that is no longer seen as pantomime.

Do your research

Always research the pantomime story you have decided to tell in order to get a general overview of the standard plot. If you have only seen *Aladdin* once, you may assume that the story you saw was the definitive one. However, this is a dangerous presumption on a single viewing. Go and see as many pantomimes as you can! Often you know that you'll be producing a pantomime at least a year in advance – so go and see pantomimes in the previous Christmas period. See what works for you and what doesn't. This is not about stealing ideas from other productions, but expanding your own knowledge base. For instance, we have probably seen about six or seven professional productions of *Aladdin* in the last few years. Only one had a flying carpet – but Joyce loved the effect so much, that she felt that when she produced it, she really wanted to incorporate that idea, even though it is rarely present.

Where to get good examples

A lot of local small-scale theatres do great pantomimes, so check out your nearest. In recent years pantomimes and their stories have often been hijacked by their celebrity stars, with the majority of the story focusing on their 'celebrity' role, rather than the narrative of the pantomime. These can be great fun, but pantomime traditions are not always at the forefront when deciding what is included.

Consistently good, traditional family pantomime is being produced in the mid-scale regional theatres up and down the country. These theatres rely on the pantomime to boost their annual box office takings, thereby supporting their other productions. Because of this they invest a huge amount of time and effort in getting it right. They will often commission a new script and employ directors and designers to create brand new productions each year. They are unable to afford named 'celebrities' but instead spend their budgets on good pantomime performers and creative staging and costumes.

After seeing a lot of pantomimes you can get to understand what you don't like, as much as what you do. For instance, having seen at least six *Jack and the Beanstalk* productions before creating our version, the appearance of the Giant had always been something of a disappointment, and, it was obvious that a lot of the audience felt the same (children don't often know how to be polite – they just look bored). This knowledge led us on to further thinking and deliberating over how to create a 'satisfying giant'. Our combined knowledge of what didn't work spurred us on to think of new ways of tackling this 'giant challenge' (*see* Chapter 10).

There are some good websites offering further explanation of the history and the elements that make up each pantomime story, an example being www.its-behind-you.com. This site gives a really useful outline of the story and expectations of each pantomime. But don't just look in one place; there are numerous versions of every pantomime story. A lot of the stories are based on fairytales or folk tales that started out as oral tales rather than in written form, so there are often lots of variations on the main story theme, any one of which might inspire.

Something we've done with every pantomime is to visit the archives of the Theatre Museum, in London, which is now part of the Victoria and Albert museum collection. Depending on the story, the museum archives have around thirty different scripts of a specific pantomime. These are mostly from the nineteenth and early twentieth centuries. Looking through them all can be difficult and time-consuming as a lot of the print is tiny, and the scripts often doubled as the programme. Some of the earlier ones were written in rhyme throughout, and many older scripts start with a 'ballet' about good and evil – both of which have little relevance to modern pantomime. What looking at these early scripts does is give an overview of some of the original approaches to particular pantomime stories. An afternoon of study will give the reader the essential traditional elements of a story, and also show where there are discrepancies and where there may be room for negotiation and originality.

The Theatre Museum also has images and

Dealing with contention

Many of the *Cinderella* scripts have an early scene where the prince is out hunting in the forest and meets Cinderella for the first time. More modern stories don't use a hunt as the setting – they have the Prince just going for a walk in the forest, or Cinderella and the Prince meeting en route to somewhere else. But in the traditional tale the hunting scene sets up the royal family (Prince Charming, King and/or Queen, and Dandini the prince's right-hand man) and their privileged lives, and contrasts them with Cinderella's rather downtrodden existence. As you make decisions on how traditional to make your pantomime, keep your audience in mind. Consider how they will react to old-fashioned ideas in a contemporary world. In this case, would a modern audience frown on a Prince Charming who went hunting?

When we were making this decision, it was the year that the hunting ban came into force, and so a hot topic of debate. As director I spoke to the writer, Joe Graham, and asked him to come up with 'a hunting scene – which wasn't a hunting scene'! His idea involved the King being a little potty, and not understanding that there was a hunting ban, which led to the whole court humouring the King by pretending to ride invisible horses, with Buttons dressed up as the fox. All of which was very silly but kept with the traditional plot, whilst adding a modern twist.

The 'mock' hunting scene from Cinderella *(actors: Gina Murray, Oliver Tompsett, Andrew Bolton, Daniel Crowder, Stephen Boswell and Madeline Appiah).*

references for set and costume from nineteenth- and early twentieth-century pantomimes, which can be a good starting point, or as an inspirational springboard for other ideas and staging possibilities.

Expectations

When you are doing your research, consider the key things that people will expect when they book this 'traditional pantomime'. For instance, Cinderella's carriage and her riding off to the ball is a key element of most productions of *Cinderella*. This doesn't mean you have to have it, but if you don't you may be disappointing a large proportion of your audience. If you decide not to have a carriage, then an alternative needs to be found for the sake of the story. Perhaps the fairy does a spell which whisks her to the ball, or perhaps it's not a carriage – it's a motorbike.

Expectations will vary amongst your audience; some people may be in their eighties, and have seen a pantomime nearly every year of their lives! You will never please everybody – but by knowing your story and what the audience expects you can avoid disappointment, and instead meet, exceed, or counter their expectations.

Time of year

Pantomimes are staged only in the Christmas period and, although none of the stories has a direct link to Christmas it is difficult to envisage it being done at any other time of year. Being family entertainment it needs to be staged at a time when the adults are not working, and Christmas is the one period in the year when workplaces close down, and the whole country has free time. Also in Britain, with our Christmas period falling within the winter, it is something to go and see on those cold dark nights. Over the years the pantomime

Tania Mathurin as Fairy Bo Peep in the finale of Jack and the Beanstalk *(lighting design by John Harris).*

23

season has been reduced. Once it used to open on Boxing Day and run through to Easter. Now the opening has been moved back to the beginning of December to take advantage of school term-time, and once New Year is over audience numbers tend to dwindle. All the glitter and sparkle seems out of place, especially once Christmas decorations are removed from people's houses.

Most pantomimes will try to make some reference to the festive season. This best fits within the finale/walk-down, where the final bows and rousing songs might have a Christmas theme. The walk-down is discussed in more detail later in this chapter.

Content suitable for all ages

With a pantomime, parents, grandparents, guardians and teachers know that they can take the children and it won't have content that might offend. These people can prepare new young visitors for some of pantomime's peculiarities by explaining what they are going to see, what kind of participation there might be, and what and when

to shout out. They know this because they have learnt the format from their own experiences. This is another good reason for sticking to established traditions, such as the 'call and response' and other audience participation, as these are handed down through the generations. If you tinker with these concepts too much it may delay or even deter the audience from entering into the participatory spirit of your pantomime.

TRADITIONAL ELEMENTS WITHIN A PANTOMIME

Good and evil entrances

The good fairy always enters from stage right, the evil baddie from stage left. We get the word 'sinister' from the French word sinistre, meaning 'left', and this tradition of the baddie coming on from the left has been around for hundreds of years. In a lot of pantomimes this convention is set

Fairy Bo Peep and Fleshcreep doing their rhyming prologue in Jack and the Beanstalk *(actors: Tania Mathurin and Peter Holdway; lighting design by John Harris).*

up right at the start. The good fairy comes on stage right and introduces herself and invites us to join in with the show and is interrupted by the evil baddie coming on stage left and telling us of his or her evil plans. Once the baddie has exited (usually with a manic laugh), the fairy assures us that all will be well as she has magic powers. They continue to use these particular entrances throughout the show.

Speaking in rhyme

As mentioned previously, truly traditional pantomimes were written in rhyme. For today's audiences this can become a little tedious, and most just have the fairy (if there is one) speaking in rhyme, and then sometimes only in her Prologue. An effective opening can involve the 'goodie' and 'baddie' battling it out in rhyme.

Audience participation

In no other form of theatre is the audience, and their continued help and rebukes, an essential ingredient of the performance. It is unique in its claim that no two performances are ever the same, as the audience are in effect another character in the plot. In pantomime the action can be taken right out into the audience and the asides can be dependent on, and be changed by, the relationship that is developed between the characters and the audience during each show. A good pantomime includes the audience in all the secrets and storylines. They know more than the individual characters and will constantly try and update the goodies on the evil goings-on, or try and put the baddies off the scent.

There is no other type of theatre where the audience are positively encouraged to shout out at the tops of their voices, often drowning out the actors on stage. The booing of the baddie can get so vociferous whole sections of dialogue go unheard (especially in schools' matinées). The actor knows when he or she is getting it right when the booing happens without any encouragement from them.

Call and response

This is when certain characters come on, introduce themselves and ask for a response from the audience. This can be as simple as 'My name's Billy. Hello!' The audience will undoubtedly do a half-hearted 'hello' and then the character will say 'I can't hear you. I said, Hello!', which usually promotes a much better response. The call and response is essential for starting off the idea that the audience are allowed to join in, and so each time it is said it should be done with equal enthusiasm. It can also be a chance to get the character's name and 'style' across to the younger children. For instance, in *Aladdin*, the first entrance of the character of Wishee Washee may go something like this:

```
WISHEE:    Wotcha kids!
AUDIENCE:  Hello...
WISHEE:    I said Wotcha kids!
AUDIENCE:  Wotcha... ?
WISHEE:    That was terrible! ... Oh,
           hang on, you don't know  who I
           am yet, do you?
AUDIENCE:  No.
WISHEE:    (COPYING THEIR TONE)
           'Naaaah' . Well I'd better
           introduce myself, hadn't I? My
           name's Wishee Washee and I'm
           Aladdin's very best mate in
           the whole wide world. He's my
           BFF. Hey, I know - whenever I
           come on, I'll say 'Wotcha
           kids' and you can say 'Wotcha
           Wishee' , OK? Let's try it.
           'Wotcha kids!'
AUDIENCE:  Wotcha Wishee.
WISHEE:    I think you can do better than
           that. I said 'Wotcha kids!'
AUDIENCE:  Wotcha Wishee!
WISHEE:    Not bad. Not bad.... But
           you're not doing the big point
           that I'm doing (HE DOES A BIG
           OVER-ARM POINT AT THE
           AUDIENCE). I need to know
           you're talking to me. (DOES A
           DE NIRO IMPRESSION.) Are you
           talking to me? Are you talking
           to me? (SHAKES THAT OFF) Where
           was I (DOING THIS WITH THE BIG
```

OVER-ARM POINT)?! Wotcha
kids! Let's try just the
people in the stalls – just
the circle – now just right up
the top in the cheap seats!
What about the ashtrays
(REFERRING TO THE THEATRE
BOXES)? Ok, now, I'm going to
try you all together – I'm
going to go off, and come back
on again and see if it works.
(HE WALKS OFF STAGE LEFT, THEN
WALKS ON NONCHALANTLY, SEES
THE AUDIENCE, DOES A DOUBLE
TAKE THEN SAYS),

WISHEE: 'Wotcha kids'

AUDIENCE: WOTCHA WISHEE!!!! (HE FALLS
            OVER FROM THE STRENGTH OF THE
            NOISE).

WISHEE: That was amazing!

This is then repeated nearly every time that character enters and can also be used on their exit too. The character can add to this a move that they do along with the call out. It could be as simple as a wave or a thumbs up, or a cooler 'street' move which looks silly when done by the comic character, and which the audience (young and less young!) can have a bit of fun trying to copy.

It is really important to use this interplay throughout the pantomime as it can become less engaging if there are long periods where the audiences are not involved, so pepper your story with short bursts of these to keep the younger audiences engaged throughout.

In our production of *Jack and the Beanstalk* we were having trouble with the call and response. We tried to find a response that used Silly Billy's name, but was easy to remember. We started with 'Oh, you are Silly Billies!' – 'No, YOU are Silly Billy!' but we weren't happy with that, and more importantly, we wanted it to be something that Silly Billy could

Dale Superville as Silly Billy, doing his 'call and response' with the audience in Jack and the Beanstalk.

use when the Giant was about, to make sure the younger children were OK and not getting too scared. A member of the company came up with 'All right kids?' – 'Not bad, Bill', said in a gruff cockney accent which, when accompanied by a cool 'rapper' stance, worked really well. It worked because it wasn't quite what the audience was expecting and because the actor doing it made it fun. It definitely diffused any scary moments and also meant the Mums and Dads tried it too!

Some productions give a call and response to every character, but this can detract from the bond created between certain characters and the audience. Generally, it is the Buttons/Silly Billy/Idle Jack comic character, and/or the dame who need to have these moments with the audience.

The audience stooge

This is when one person in the audience is singled out near the start of the evening and then referred to periodically throughout the show. This can be done when the comic character is establishing their call and response. Below is an example from *Dick Whittington and his Cat* where Tommy the Cat was also the comic character:

```
CAT:       Whenever I come on I'll say
           'Wotcha Cats!' And I want you
           to say 'Wotcha Tommy – Miao!'
           Shall we try it? (GOES OFF.
           COMES ON AGAIN, DOES DOUBLE
           TAKE AS IF SEEING THEM FOR THE
           FIRST TIME.) Wotcha Cats!
AUDIENCE:  Wotcha Tommy – Miao!
CAT:       That was brilliant! Hang on,
           I just realized you know my
           name, but I don't know any of
           yours. So after 3 can you all
           shout out your name? OK,
           1,2,3 –(AS THE AUDIENCE
           SHOUTS OUT THEIR NAMES, CAT
           LOOKS AS IF HE'S LISTENING TO
           THE DIFFERENT PARTS OF THE
           AUDITORIUM.)
           Great. I think I got all of
           those... except... yours,
```

```
sir. Yes you, trying to sink
down into your chair. What's
your name? Malcolm? Wotcha
Malcolm! (HOPEFULLY MALCOLM
SAYS, 'Wotcha Tommy – Miao!')
```

The actor can then go on to find out some information about 'Malcolm' such as what his job is, where he lives etc. This can then be referred to at different points in the story, and each time the comic character comes on and does his call and response, he can also do a special one for the 'stooge' afterwards.

If it is the dame finding the stooge, she can spot him in her opening scene, and because she is often single and looking for love, 'Malcolm' can seem her ideal man. She can flirt with him every time she comes on, and she can check he likes her outfit. At the end, if she gets together with someone she can then apologize to Malcolm for betraying him. If the stooge is a woman, the dame can talk to her in a gossipy way about men: 'Oh we know about men don't we, Enid? I mean I've been married five times, and you've had more men than hot dinners haven't you? And doesn't the Emperor look gorgeous! Is he your type, Enid?' – that sort of thing.

Tommy the cat and Dick chatting with the audience stooge in **Dick Whittington and his Cat** *(actors: Dale Superville and Tom Bradley).*

Who makes a good audience stooge?

The stooge can be anyone who the actors think will be 'up for it'. It is best if this is not a young person (they often get far too embarrassed), and if they are that bit older, there is more chance that they have been to pantomimes before and know the drill. With a school audience a senior teacher is the best bet. Some actors peek at the audience before the show to try and suss out a good stooge; sometimes the front of house staff pinpoint someone they think will join in.

They need to be sitting somewhere where most of the audience can see them, this usually means one of the first few rows. Some audience members book these seats on purpose, in fact a line that is often said by actors to an embarrassed stooge is,

'Well, Jane, if you didn't want to get picked on, you shouldn't have got seats at the front. You'll know for next year now, won't you?' Once the stooge is picked out, the deputy stage manager should write the name on a bright post-it note, and attach it in a prominent position on the Prompt Desk for the rest of the show. After a few weeks, and with forty or so shows under their belts, your actors will appreciate the quick reminder just before they go on.

Cross-dressing

Cross-dressing is something that has been around in pantomime from the late nineteenth century and now into the twenty-first century, and is what helps separate pantomime from other seasonal family shows. Where else in contemporary theatre

The heroine Alice Fitzwarren disguising herself as Bob the Sailor to smuggle herself aboard ship, hence the unusual addition of classic principal boy tunic and false moustache (Alice played by Sia Kiwa).

Peter Shorey as Widow Twankey in Aladdin.

do you have a mother who is actually a man and a son that is actually a girl, ending up with partners that are true to their sex and everyone accept this as the norm?

The principal boy

It is interesting that some of the reasons why pantomime cross-dressing came about might appear today as quite tame. The principal boy came from the Music Hall acts of stars such as

Cross-dressing in the extreme

Because of the established presence of cross dressing in pantomime, it can be used to create original twists to the normal storylines. In our version of *Dick Whittington and his Cat*, in Act 2, the goodies have to get into disguise to rescue Neptune from the clutches of King Rat. They were all disguised as 'teenage girlfriends' of Neptune's daughter. The dame was scarily disguised as a sixteen-year-old 'streetwise schoolgirl'; Dick was loosely disguised as a young petulant girl with blond curls and ra-ra skirt. Then

Alice Fitzwarren, who had already disguised herself as Bob the Sailor (at the end of Act 1) was now pretending to be a cheerleader (a double cross-dress), retaining Bob's moustache. Finally Tommy the Cat, who had previously been disguised as a parrot, was now disguised as a fish (cross-species dressing). Believe it or not, this all made perfect sense within the narrative, and it added to the fun for both the company and the audiences.

A feast of cross dressing in Dick Whittington and his Cat *(actors: Howard Coggins, Alice Jackson, Natasha Cox, Jeff Nicholson, Sia Kiwa, Tom Bradley and Dale Superville).*

Vesta Tilley and Marie Lloyd who were some of the first to don the principal boy outfit. Their clothing was often quite risqué for those times, with their characters (the heroes), appearing as tunic-clad youths with lots of leg on show, thus bypassing laws and perceived prudery about women showing too much of their bodies.

Cross-dressing in pantomime has changed in the last few decades: the principal boy is less used now, and is often replaced by an attractive male youth. This does make more sense in pantomimes such as Cinderella, where the 'falling in love' aspect is a major part of the plot. Using a handsome young man (and on commercial pantomimes, heartthrobs from TV) appears to pull in a wider audience, especially teenage girls. But, where the hero is more heroic than romantic, in such pantomimes as *Jack and the Beanstalk*, it is perhaps a shame that we don't see as many women thigh slapping, striking macho poses, and striding around in knee-length boots. This camp form of masculinity balances really well with the dame.

Current references

Interestingly you do not have to look far into mainstream pop culture for examples of female cross-dressing in this era of post-feminism. Cultural icons and role models such as Madonna, Kylie and Lady Ga Ga use it as one of their weapons of celebrity, whether for a fleeting image or sensationalism. In pantomime it is surviving political correctness and remaining at the heart of pantomime as a feisty, independent and glamorous character.

Celia Perkins: set and costume designer

The dame

The concept of the dame began when certain Music Hall comedians of the late nineteenth century began adding female characters in their acts and these were then transposed into the pantomime dame. In these early manifestations they were dressed as drab, working-class old women, complete with grey hair tied up in a bun, rather than the absurdly clothed frisky and weirdly glamorous creations we often see today. These characters will be explained in more detail in later chapters.

The moral

Morals in pantomime are usually very strong and clear-cut. You have intrinsically good characters and intrinsically bad ones. These are clearly defined, and good must always overcome evil by the end of Act 2. The conquering of evil is met when the baddie (or baddies) of the piece are persuaded to repent their evil ways and become good. This is sometimes a personal recognition, but more frequently accomplished with a wave of the good fairy's wand.

Walk-down/finale

Appropriately, the last traditional element discussed is the walk-down and finale. It requires the entire company to change into completely new outfits to walk downstage, take their bows and then conclude with a medley of songs (usually Christmas hits). It may seem an obvious thing to cut, but the pantomime will feel incomplete if this is lost. The audiences love the chance to cheer, applaud and boo (the baddie), and they love the spectacle of the highly elaborate and be-jewelled costumes that accompany this scene.

All pantomimes have to have a happy ending so the walk-down/finale can offer this resolution. The plot for this scene is usually centred around the marriage of the romantic central characters and is set up at the end of the previous scene by either the dame or the comic character, who invite the whole audience to the 'wedding'. This leads into the finale and a procession of all the characters entering from upstage (usually down a staircase), stepping forward and taking their bows, then peeling off to the two sides of the stage as the next characters enter. The dame will be decked out in the most extravagant of her outfits and the hero and heroine dressed in sparkly pantomime wedding attire. The whole company then joins together for a finale song or medley that should have the audience clapping and singing along as the show

Kieran Buckeridge and Dale Superville as Adorabella and Fruitella (the Ugly Sisters) in the finale of Cinderella.

ends and the curtain falls.

To give this scene more narrative value the bows can be interspersed with dialogue, usually tying up all the loose ends and giving every character a happy ending. Even the baddie has usually repented and will be paired off with one of the other characters.

Using traditions

There is no hard and fast rule as to which or how many of pantomime's traditions you should incorporate into present-day productions. The decision of what to keep and what to ignore is helped by a good level of research and seeing as many pantomimes as you can, in order to build your own views of what makes a good traditional family pantomime. When seeing other shows, take careful note of the reactions of the audiences to the action and the different scenes. Especially look for when the young audience gets fidgety and bored, or at the other end of the scale, noisy and totally engaged. The audience is the best barometer to decide the success of a particular scene or moment, and can help you to decide what traditions will work for your own production.

31

3 STRUCTURING YOUR SCRIPT

So, the title has been decided, you know the audience you're going to be writing for, and you've considered how traditional you want to make it. Now you need to think about how you are going to tell your story.

GETTING STARTED

Initially, when you start writing a pantomime, it's good to leap in and get writing all your favourite bits – the bits that are already in your mind. It might be a great idea for the dame's first entrance, or how the dialogue may go for the heroine and baddie when they first meet. Whatever, this burst of writing is good, and will help get some ideas down. For instance our scene where Dick Whittington meets Tommy the Cat was first scribbled down in January, at about eleven o'clock at night in a very small notebook, whilst waiting for the last train home, and a lot of that initial dialogue stayed in the final show.

However, after the initial flood of ideas, start thinking in a more pragmatic, practical way, because without thinking about the overall structure of the piece in the early stages, you risk getting yourself into knots, which can be difficult to untie.

OPPOSITE: *Joyce Branagh working on changes to the script for* **Jack and the Beanstalk.**

List synopsis

A good way to begin the structure of your story is to make a 'list synopsis': a very basic list of what happens in the story. If you have picked one of the more traditional tales you may already have the basics of your story in your head, but it is still good to see it written down. It may look something like this:

Jack and the Beanstalk
1. Jack and his mother are poor.
2. The Giant is terrorizing the village.
3. His henchman collects rent from all the villagers, but Jack's family can't afford to pay.
4. Jack sells his cow in exchange for some magic beans.
5. Mum is angry and throws out the beans.
6. Overnight the beans grow into an enormous beanstalk.
7. Jack climbs the beanstalk and goes to the Giant's castle.
8. The Giant is asleep and Jack steals a hen that lays golden eggs and a harp that sings.
9. As he is making his escape the Giant wakes up, and chases Jack down the beanstalk.
10. Once Jack is at the bottom of the beanstalk he chops down the beanstalk and the Giant

crashes to the ground.

11. Jack and family are rich and live happily ever after.

Questions

The next step is to question some of these basic ideas. Consider your basic story – there may be some aspects of the traditional tale that need clarifying or changing in your version. Look back at the list synopsis and ask questions of each of the points you've made:

1. Do we need to know why Jack and his mum are poor?
2. Why is the Giant terrorizing the village? Is he just pure evil? Or is there a reason?
3. Why does the henchman work for the Giant? Fear? Or...?
4. Who sells Jack the beans? Is it a goodie who wants him to have the magic? Or a baddie who wants to steal his cow?
5. Why does Jack want to go up the beanstalk if he knows the Giant is up there?!
6. Is it OK that Jack steals the Giant's hen and harp? Is the stealing justified in any way?
7. Does Jack kill the Giant? And is that OK?
8. Is it just the money that makes them happy? If not, what else happens?
9. Do they get the cow back somehow?!

Options

Not all the questions need answers because pantomime doesn't have to be logical, but by asking the questions, as a writer, you make sure you know where you are heading with the story, and where there are holes or options that you may wish to follow. Options/ideas may be something along the lines of:

1. Perhaps they were rich before the Giant came? Or perhaps we just accept that they are poor?
2. Perhaps the Giant isn't bad? Perhaps he's under the spell of the henchman?
3. So – perhaps the henchman (Fleshcreep) is in charge!
4. Perhaps Fleshcreep buys the cow with beans, not realizing that they are magic? Or they are ordinary and then made 'magic' by a fairy...
5. Perhaps Jack's friend and/or girlfriend gets kidnapped, which is why he goes up the beanstalk – to rescue them? Or Jack could get kidnapped and the girlfriend could go and rescue him!
6. Perhaps the hen and the harp belong to Jack's mum and were stolen? Or belong to his girlfriend's mum and so returning them would be good for his marriage plans?
7. Perhaps if the Giant is basically a nice bloke, Jack can take his revenge on Fleshcreep instead. And maybe not death – something daft/humiliating...?
8. If Jack has rescued his girlfriend or friend, then being safe (as well as the cash) makes them happy. Perhaps Jack needed cash to marry the girl? Perhaps his mother needed the cash to follow her dream of being... something? (Celebrity chef? DJ? Mayor?)
9. We must get the cow back somehow by the end of the story!!

Most or all of these ideas may get ditched along the way, but they open up creative avenues that stay within the basic storyline. Use your research and knowledge of the different approaches to the traditional story. For instance, most of the Jack and the Beanstalk plots have a love interest, so

---

Talking initial ideas through with the designer

In our earliest meeting for *Jack and the Beanstalk* – eleven months before the production that Christmas, both Keith and I had independently thought that we didn't like the idea of Jack stealing. Also, we thought that we would quite like to create the Giant as a 'secret goodie'.

We were also keen on the idea of the beanstalk talking, and we definitely wanted Jack to be able to climb the beanstalk 'for real', which ultimately meant it probably couldn't be chopped down.

Even knowing these small points early on helped in the overall development and structure of the script.

Joyce Branagh

'rescuing the girl', and a 'happy-ever-after wedding' may seem definite plot-points, rather than an option.

If at this stage, the writer/director and designer have a meeting, some of these initial ideas can be thrown around. The designer can start to add some of their initial thoughts about the story and the design, which might affect how the story develops.

Once the 'team' has had a few initial ideas the writer then needs to start making decisions about the rough plan of the story. Though it doesn't need to be in great detail at this stage, it will need to take into consideration who the characters are (*see* Chapter 6). Generally speaking, the pantomime story is broken up into a series of scenes, each of which tells a section of the story. A rough plan is similar to the list synopsis already discussed, but goes into more detail about what happens, and it will clearly show your version of the story.

Thinking technically
A pantomime is always large and technical. It will undoubtedly involve music and songs, large scenic elements and moments that you want to make exciting through the use of 'reveals' or 'magic'. This means that when you are thinking about the structure of the story, it is a good idea to think with some of the practicalities to the fore. This might seem like something that would stifle creativity, but actually, these 'rules' can help when it comes to writing the dialogue. It's not just a blank sheet of paper staring at you, but a plan with goals.

For instance, if you want Prince Charming and Cinderella to meet in the forest, does it make sense to start with everyone in the forest? Or, is it better to have an establishing scene in the kitchen and then go to the forest and back to the kitchen? If these ideas are discussed with the designer there may be very practical reasons why the forest will need to be the opening scene. Maybe it is too difficult and time-consuming to move back and forth between kitchen and forest?

If something like this seems to be ruining the initial idea for the story, try thinking about it in a new way. Could the initial scene be a frontcloth scene (set in front of a downstage painted cloth), which then lifts to reveal the forest? Could Buttons and Cinderella be walking through the audience? Is there another place/setting that Cinders could meet the Prince? Often something that at first seems like a difficulty can prompt a radical new idea, such as the new 'garden' scene which we developed in *Cinderella* (discussed in Chapter 8). 'Necessity is the mother of invention', after all!

Many pantomime productions will contain lots of music and songs to help move the story along. If this is the style chosen, then structure your pantomime story with the music in mind from the beginning, and perhaps include no more than one song per scene. Think about whether the story needs a full company dance at a crucial narrative moment or whether it is the appropriate time for a solo (see Chapter 9 for more details on music and song).

Initial outline
Once some of the design ideas and the technical considerations have been incorporated into the initial story plan, it is good to put together a scene-by-scene outline for the whole pantomime. Some sections will be clearer than others at first, but this is a good starting point for writer and designer to talk through the possible challenges, and for the designer to start thinking about the best way to get from scene to scene smoothly.

Below is an example of a scene outline for *Dick Whittington and his Cat*, which was produced at Watford Palace Theatre. The outline was sent to Keith as designer in February, a full ten months prior to the show that Christmas. You can see that the storyline for Act 2 contains a lot more question marks and undecided details, but provided a good starting point for discussion and collaboration.

Dick Whittington – scene outline
1. Prologue: Frontcloth – Fairy Bow-Bells and King Rat explain their enmity.
2. Watford Landmark – The Palace of Varieties? Milestone saying '21 miles to London' (not sure about this – perhaps we should get straight onto London – but like the Watford angle). Dick arrives in Watford having travelled all the way from.... Fairy sees the cat

and decides to provide Dick with a friend. She casts a spell on the cat. Dick sees that the cat is hungry and offers him half his tuna sandwich – the cat starts speaking and chatting to the audience. They become instant friends and decide to travel to London together.

3. London Street – Dick arrives in London, penniless and disappointed about the pavements (maybe outside Fitzwarren's shop) – possibly London town number 'Maybe it's because I'm a Londoner'/'Lambeth Walk' – possibly led by Sarah as Pearly Queen. Lord Mayor of London leaves in a tizzy because of the rat problem. Dick tries to get a job but fails. (Gotta Dance! But gotta sweep/chop/...) They meet Idle Jack (who keeps falling asleep) and Alderman Fitzwarren who needs more staff – they have a rat problem. Tommy says he will get Dick a job – but everyone acts as if they can't hear him. A cat can't be talking! He suggests that Dick get him some clothing – once he is wearing boots everyone listens. On Tommy's recommendation, Alderman Fitzwarren hires Jack – but says there's no room for a cat. Tommy prepares to go. Sidekick Rat celebrates. Tommy fights Sidekick Rat, and wins – much to King Rat's dismay. Alderman Fitzwarren hires Tommy too. Dick meets Alice – they fall in love.

4. Frontcloth – Dick and Alice have romantic song. King Rat (with the 'help' of Sidekick Rat) explains that he will get Dick – Fairy assures us she will protect Dick.

5. Fitzwarren's Stores – The shop sells all sorts of exciting things...! Dick and Cat are shown the 'job' by Sarah and Idle Jack.

6. Slosh scene?/Cooking scene. Alice tells Dick that she wants to go to sea and be a sailor, but Dad says she can't – she's a girl. Then Alderman puts cash in safe. King Rat and Sidekick sneak in, hypnotize Idle Jack/Tommy/Sarah/ somehow and put cash in Dick's bag. The crime is discovered and Dick and Cat are chucked out.

7. Frontcloth – King Rat gloats, singing a song with his rat tribe (Cool cat?/Cool for Rats?). Fairy Bow-Bells is going to work out how to get

Dick back to London.

8. Watford landmark – The Palace of Varieties, and milestone? Dick is back in Watford. They talk about staying in Watford, as they like it! Fairy Bow-Bells makes the London bells ring extra loud. Dick and Cat comment on the fact that they can hear bells so far away.... Then they realize that the bells are saying 'Turn again Whittington, Lord Mayor of London'. Dick decides he should go back, but Tommy points out their situation – and suggests that Dick gets rich first before returning. They decide to travel the seas to foreign lands to make their fortune.

9. Frontcloth – Dick and Tommy sing a song about going to sea (or seaside Music Hall medley?). As they leave King Rat says that he will make sure Dick's new adventure fails; Fairy Bow Bells says that she'll look after them – she reveals a captain's hat and large beard....

10. By the docks/on board ship – Alice, Alderman Fitzwarren, Sarah and Idle Jack are by the docks watching the *Saucy Sally* being loaded. Idle Jack and Sarah are going on the voyage to pick up exotic goods. Alice wants to go too, but Alderman says she must stay home as she's just a girl. When Alderman Fitzwarren heads off, Alice changes (Bucks Fizz style!) into boys' clothes and announces to Sarah and Jack that she is Bob. The Captain turns up (Fairy in disguise), Jack and Tommy ask the Captain if they can work on ship. He agrees. They all think Bob looks rather familiar but shrug it off and all set sail....

11. Saucy Sally (can be part of previous scene). As ship sails off we realize that King Rat is on board. He and his sidekick and little rats sink the ship somehow. Fairy lets us know that she has a cunning plan as the ship sinks... (It's the end of the world as we know it, but I feel fine...?).

INTERVAL

1. Frontcloth Fairy assures us that our heroes are OK!

2. Under the sea – 'Octopus's garden', certainly a

'musical number' – maybe a medley. Maybe The King of Morocco and his Daughter save our heroes in a Yellow Submarine...? Not sure yet....

3. Frontcloth – King Rat is annoyed that Dick has escaped but has a plan, which he shares with his sidekick.

4. Ghost scene – on the beach or in the palace there's a ghost/scary creature 'behind-you' scene. (This could even happen under the sea before rescue. Or the King could be King Neptune, the whole second half is spent under the sea, and they bring back treasures of pearls....)

5. Frontcloth – Fairy (half in Captain disguise) keeps us abreast of what's happening, and probably sings a song....

6. In the Palace – The heroes are invited to a feast(?) There is a song but chaos ensues when the rats come. Eventually Tommy, Dick and 'Bob' (with the 'help' of Sarah, Idle Jack the King and his Daughter) dispatch all the rats. Dick captures King Rat. King offers Dick his daughter and half his wealth. Dick turns down the daughter – though Idle Jack doesn't! Dick says he is still in love with Alice. Bob's identity is revealed. Dick and Alice are to be married. Now Dick is rich he says he will build schools and hospitals. They head home....

7. Songsheet.

8. Wedding – at the wedding Queen Victoria comes along (if we set it definitely in 1908 – we can make a joke about this), she has heard of Dick's good works. She makes Dick Lord Mayor of London.

A well-planned and structured scene outline can be invaluable before you really get down to writing. A writer I spoke to recently likened story structure to pegging out the washing: imagine your story is a

A frontcloth scene in Dick Whittington and his Cat *where Alice sings of her love for* Dick Whittington, *whilst a major scene change is occurring upstage (actors: Alice Jackson, Natasha Cox and Sia Kiwa).*

washing line. Your first peg would be your first opening scene – the last peg your finale. Then you need to think about key moments and put those pegs in at the appropriate point on the line. Then when you come to writing, you can pluck down a peg and the accompanying scene and know roughly what you're aiming to achieve ('Ah! So today I am going to write how King Rat plans to blow up the *Saucy Sally!*'), and instead of a huge sheet of blank paper staring at you, you have a plan. Or at least a washing line full of pegs ....

STRUCTURES

Frontcloth scenes

Pantomimes, especially the more traditional ones, need frontcloth scenes in between major set changes. These scenes need to be thought about and put into the structure of the piece in advance. They are there to give the cast and crew enough time to change the set and costumes. In a good pantomime script, these scenes are not just scene-change 'padding' – they are integral parts of the plot, but don't require as much playing space. For instance, they are often ideal moments for a story-update from the fairy, or a fairy/baddie word battle, or a point where the hero or heroine sings a ballad to let us know they've fallen in love.

Because of the special relationship that exists between the actors and the audience, and because these frontcloth scenes are so far downstage, they can be a great way of being more intimate and direct with the audience. In your script structure it is important to use these moments well.

Prologue

Many pantomimes have a prologue, and this is often a chance to introduce the forces of good and evil, as explained previously. Usually these are staged as a 'frontcloth scene'; some pantomimes skip the prologue and go straight to the opening scene.

Opening scene

This can start with a big song and dance, and after this, or as a break mid-song, all the main protagonists can be introduced. The audience needs to meet the hero or heroine and find out their main dilemma/obstacle to happiness. For example:

- Cinderella's Ugly Sisters are horrible to her, and she has to do all the housework.
- Jack is poor and lives with his mum, and their cow, in a village that lives in fear of a Giant.
- Dick comes to London to make his fortune, but finds that the streets aren't paved with gold.

Work out what the main dilemma/obstacle is for your central character and get the information across to the audience as soon as you can.

We also need to meet and get to know your comic character (Buttons/Silly Billy/Idle Jack) and establish the call and response.

Where there is a pantomime dame, it is important to get to know her in this first scene. She may also have some banter with the audience, and will probably interact with the comic character and hero/heroine.

Towards the end of this first scene (or in the next scene) your central character may be faced with a further dilemma, for example:

- Cinderella has met a nice man, but won't be able to go to the ball to see him again.
- Fleshcreep has raised the rent, which means that Jack's family must sell their cow.
- Dick has fallen for Alice, but how will he get to marry her as he has no money?

There may be other secondary dilemmas too. In Dick Whittington, the Fitzwarrens usually have a 'rat problem' that Dick's cat seems to quickly solve. Often, Prince Charming in Cinderella needs to marry soon or lose the Kingdom.

Plot information

It may seem difficult to have so much 'plot' happening so early, but pantomimes need the energy of their set-up to drive them forward. It is important to explain the 'problems' as straightforwardly as possible, so that everyone in the theatre, even the younger members of the

The opening scene in Jack and the Beanstalk, *and the moment where the town hears the Giant's threatening voice (actors: Alice Jackson, Martine Burt, Natasha Cox, Richard Ashton, Dale Superville, Ricardo Coke-Thomas and the junior chorus; lighting design by John Harris).*

audience, knows what's at stake. The lovely thing with pantomime is that this can often be stated quite boldly:

```
KING:     Hubert, you must marry.
PRINCE:   Marry?
KING:     Yes, and before your twenty-
          first birthday.
PRINCE:   But, I'm twenty-one at the
          end of the month!
KING:     Exactly! Better get a move on
          hadn't you! (goes to leave)
PRINCE:   But Dad, that's daft!
KING:     Daft is it? Well, I don't
          think it's daft to lose my
          Kingdom.
PRINCE:   Lose the Kingdom? But -
KING:     If you don't marry by the time
          you're twenty-one, the whole
          Kingdom will be mysteriously
          inherited by Simon Cowell.
DANDINI:  Simon Cowell?
KING:     Yes!
PRINCE:   NO!
KING:     Exactly! Which is why I have
          organized - a Grand Ball.
          Find a nice girl at the ball
          and marry her. Otherwise...
DANDINI:  Simon Cowell becomes King of
          Windy Bottoms!
KING:     Exactly! Not a nice thought,
          is it son. Find a bride! Windy
          Bottoms is depending on you.
```

Once you have set up your various characters' obstacles, then you can proceed with the rest of the story.

Further scenes

As you move through your story, make sure that each scene progresses the plot. Quite a lot of action needs to happen in a relatively short space of time.

Whilst there are definitely times when the story can take a back seat, a well-written pantomime takes every opportunity to forward the story. So, there might be a slosh scene cooking moment, but it might end with the baddie getting the pie in his face, which gives him a motive for revenge. Or, Widow Twankey might lose the Emperor's pants in a silly scene in the laundry, which might perhaps give you a nice final moment when she hands them back at the end of the show.

If you make every moment of the story count, you are more likely to keep your audience involved in the world you are creating.

With the more popular titles like Cinderella or Dick Whittington, there are strong storylines and structures to adhere to, as well as certain scene expectations. Again, research is a great tool. Find out what the norm is for your particular tale. If there are scenes that 'should' be there, it's good to know this, so you can manage, organize and possibly surpass people's expectations in your particular telling of the story.

End of Act 1

Whatever the story, you need to send the audience out for the interval on a high note, and also one where they need to come back to find out what happens next. For instance, Cinderella generally ends the first Act by going off to the ball in her carriage. This is a magical highpoint, but we also know that there is the twelve o'clock deadline coming up!

Often the audience needs to be left with a cliff-hanger, such as Dick Whittington's ship sinking, but what will happen to the crew? Or, Jack is going up the Beanstalk and will have to face the Giant! Whatever it is, you need to make sure that the younger ones are interested but not too terrified to come back. Sometimes the choice of music can help. If our hero is singing away merrily, there can't be too much to worry about, can there? Or perhaps the good fairy can let everyone know she's going to make sure our hero is all right. Whatever happens, it is often good to see a few friendly waves, and the dame or comic character saying 'See you later' as the curtain falls.

Beginning of Act 2

Everyone (adults and children alike) begin to sit down to watch the second act in a slightly distracted way (full of ice-cream, playing with toys, etc.). You need to grab them straight away, and whisk them back into the story. This may start with a quick reminder from the fairy of what's happening, but after this short re-introduction, the main start of Act 2 must be full of life and energy, and will probably be a musical number. This section always used to be a 'ballet' performed by the young chorus, which can work quite well, but needs to be kept punchy and short.

The second half of a pantomime is often shorter than the first and you'll have a lot of story to get in. It tends to have fewer detours within the plot, as our heroes are in peril! The goodies should be concentrating on the main point: overturning the baddie's evil plans.

Most stories have a moment towards the middle of Act 2 where it looks as if the baddie will win. This is great, as the more difficult and unlikely it is that our heroes will triumph, the more we want them to, and the more heroic they look when they finally do. Make sure therefore, you have at least one moment when everyone looks a bit dispirited and they can't see a way out of their predicament.

Turning point into 'happy ever after'

This can occur in a number of different ways: the fairy can cast a spell, the heroes and heroines can fight the baddie, the baddie's sidekicks can swap to the goodie's side – any combination (or all) of these could happen. What these moments should try and create is an almost involuntary cheer from the audience (even the adults) when finally good seems to be winning over evil.

Loose ends

If you have started various storylines in a pantomime, it feels much more satisfying if they are all tied up neatly in the end: 'punishing' the baddies, getting the hero and heroine together, solving whatever was the initial problem or dilemma that you started out with.

There is also a tradition of pairing nearly everyone off by the end, which can seem forced,

*Jack climbing the beanstalk to rescue Jill from the clutches of the Giant
(Ricardo Coke-Thomas as Jack; lighting design by John Harris).*

but this can often add to the humour of it all. We can't see why the King suddenly finds the dame attractive, but we are all in on the absurdity of it, so it's OK. Often the last main scene needs to be concerned with getting the hero and heroine to finally kiss, and tying up other loose ends may seem to get in the way of their romantic moment. If this is the case, sometimes the walk-down/finale can become a little 'tying things together' scene in its own right.

Mixing it up

As your script starts to take shape, it's good to look at the mix and order of the scenes. By keeping a

Princess Baldroubadour held captive by the wicked Abanazar, with Wishee Washee hidden behind a piece of set (actors: Rachel Grimshaw, John Alastair and Dale Superville; lighting design by John Harris).

good mix (intimate, full company, slapstick and romantic) you will hopefully keep all areas of the audience entertained.

Make sure that there is not a huge section of pure 'plot' dialogue. The younger audience will lose interest. If you seem to have a large expositional section, have a look at another approach. Does all of this information need to be given at this moment? Could we have learnt some of it earlier? Or could some of it come out in the next scene? Does it all have to be 'said'? Could you show that your hero has fallen in love, rather than have them tell someone? Might a song be used to convey some of the information? Is there a way that physical humour could be used within the scene? Or perhaps some audience participation could be introduced?

If a younger audience is primed before a scene (asked to listen or look out for something by the comic character) they are often more attentive in

Queen Victoria stops the finale to make Dick Whittington Lord Mayor of London (actors: Howard Coggins and Tom Bradley).

the following dialogue-driven sections. This patient attention then needs to be rewarded by checking back on the information with them, and being suitably astonished by their cleverness!

Try to make sure the music is spaced throughout the piece; brief but frequent is often a good idea. Similarly, audience participation needs to be evenly spread throughout the show. It can be great fun, but it does get very noisy (especially 'behind you' moments). If there is too much loud

audience participation, or if it happens all in one go, it may make your adult audience start to wish they were somewhere else....

Jokes

If you have a very wide age range within the audience, make sure that in each scene you mix the type of humour you're using. Research and find lots of short jokes, of all different sorts and styles, with different age/cultural references. Have them to hand as you write, surround yourself with lists, books and notepads. Make sure these jokes include visual, physical, topical, puns, and daft kids' ones (Knock-Knock, Doctor-Doctor), then you can pepper them throughout the script as you write.

BEGINNING IN EARNEST

If you have a good, detailed, scene-by-scene structural outline of your story, it makes things a lot easier when it comes to actually writing the dialogue. This should include the characters, the information that needs to be got over, songs that might be sung, and an idea of how the scene might end, or segue into the next one. With an outline in place, in theory, you just need to join the dots, though of course in practice it's a lot more difficult. There will be head-scratching, and scenes that just won't come, but if you have spent time on the structure and talking through how this might all work on stage with the designer, then you at least have something to hang your ideas on.

Testing your script

Once you have got a first draft of your script you will almost certainly have to hand it immediately to the designer who will need to start working from it as soon as they can. Getting feedback from the designer is a great idea, but also find another outside eye to read the script, someone who doesn't know your outline so well. They might be able to spot problems or weaknesses in the plot or the story-telling more readily than someone who is closer to the script. This needs to be someone you trust to be honest, who can draw your attention to areas that are working less well or are confusing, as well as letting you know the sections that had them giggling!

After this feedback, then make subsequent drafts. Most pantomimes will need four or five drafts by the time rehearsals start. Often it is good to write a draft and then not read it for a week or so. This distance can help you spot the problems you might have overlooked due to being too close to it. This, alongside having helpful colleagues to give

---

Listen very carefully, I shall say this only once

When I handed in my first draft of *Jack and the Beanstalk* to Brigid Larmour, the Artistic Director of Watford Palace Theatre, she mentioned that she didn't think the personality of the beanstalk was as good as it could be. I was very proud of the talking beanstalk – I'd made it American, and thought that this gave it the feel of the plant 'Audrey' from *Little Shop of Horrors*. But this was obviously not coming across. The American voice in such a typically English setting seemed to jar. I then spoke to my designer Keith and he said, 'Well of course it needs to be a French Bean!' – a terrible joke, but a great idea. I then made the Beanstalk speak with a French accent, which lent itself to a bit of silliness and meant that we could make allusions to the TV programme 'Allo 'Allo, and Keith could give the design of the beanstalk a French twist – all much better than my original idea, but one that I wouldn't have come up with if I had been working in isolation.   *Joyce Branagh*

---

you feedback, will get better clarity in the storyline and the writing.

If you can (when you've still got time before rehearsals to make changes), get a group of people to read the script out loud. At Watford Palace Theatre the Youth Theatre did this for us in September. It was a great way of testing how the script sounded, where it got lots of laughs, and where it got bogged down in plot. You could also tell quite easily which characters were written clearly by how easily the young actors got to grips with them. The young people were good at giving their feedback too, and it was a fun way to spend an afternoon, before heading back to the computer with a heap of notes ....

What you are creating is of course is a new piece of writing, and you will only be able to tell where your script truly works and where it doesn't in the rehearsal room, which we will look at later in Chapter 11.

The French beanstalk talking to Jack for the first time in Jack *and the Beanstalk (Ricardo Coke-Thomas as Jack; Alice Jackson as the puppeteer and voice of the beanstalk; lighting design by John Harris).*

4 TRADITIONAL SET PIECES AND PANTOMIME GAGS

These are often stand-alone moments, and most hark back to the origins of pantomime and Music Hall. By no means modern, they have been tried and tested with audiences for years, proving their value to engage and entertain, and are key elements of any pantomime. Whilst you are under no obligation to include them, they are worth considering, since leaving them out can lead to disappointment.

It is really important that the design understands how these set pieces function and the comic timing that is required to make them both possible and funny. This is something that can be achieved by looking back through archives or talking to performers or theatres that have staged these gags previously. New interpretations can be done, but only once you understand the history, the action, and the punchlines.

THE SLOSH OR SLOP SCENE

The slosh scene is where things get really messy. They take time to rehearse and plan but for some, especially the younger children, they are the essence of pantomime. Their messiness can make them expensive to stage due to large amounts of running props, and crew needed to set up and clear

these scenes. However, the fun and silliness that can be derived from seeing the characters covered in gloop makes it money well spent.

They might form part of a scene involving cooking a pie. It could be that it explodes, or the finished pie gets pushed into someone's face. Perhaps it is a scene where ingredients for the cooking end up on someone's face rather than in the bowl. Sometimes a cake has already been made, and covered in lots of cream which the comic character then tries to get someone to sit on, but ends up sitting or being pushed onto it him or herself. It may also involve a 'getting ready to go out' scene and so is about make-up and face-powder going horribly wrong.

Any slosh scene cream or any 'gunk' that touches an actor needs to be checked. Find out if the actors have any allergies. If the substance goes anywhere near the eyes (which it frequently does), it must be safe for this, and if it goes near their mouths or they consume it, obviously it needs to be edible. You will need to do 'slosh tests' to establish how runny/gloopy you want it. If artificially coloured, it mustn't stain skin or clothing. Eggs look great but are terrible to clear up quickly, and during a long run can end up making the whole backstage area smell, as can substances such as

OPPOSITE: *Christopher Robert with his 'impressive' cream cake in a scene from* Jack and the Beanstalk.

47

Tommy the Cat covered up in one of Sarah the Cook's dressing gowns (washable) during the slosh scene in Dick Whittington and his Cat *(actors: Dale Superville and Howard Coggins).*

instant dessert mixes. It all needs thorough researching and testing.

The actors will need time before their next entrance to get the gunk off, so look at where the slosh scene comes in the story to allow for this. Clothing for performers in these scenes will need to be washable or wipe clean to make them last for the entire run.

Dependent on the amount of slop, a specific floor cloth may need to be created to enable the spillage to be cleared quickly (by simply removing this splattered floor in the scene change). What this is made of can depend on the type of slop, but in most cases is best made from vinyl as it can be taken out to the back of the theatre and hosed down and/or mopped in preparation for the next performance. It could be as simple as a coloured plastic tarpaulin, or a specifically designed and painted floor.

From the various types of slosh scene, find out which works best for your story (as you probably only want to include one in the show). Think about your available facilities, budget, space, rehearsal time, etc. All slosh scenes work best if, before whatever activity they are embarking on, the idea is set up that 'we mustn't make a mess …'! Below are descriptions of a few of the tried-and-tested approaches to the slosh scene.

Cooking scene

These are the most popular form of slosh scene as most storylines can squeeze a kitchen scene somewhere into the plot. There are some standard jokes which always appear, and involve flour getting everywhere. They are normally led by the dame with the comic character being an able assistant, but of course getting everything wrong. The scenes tend to start with the need for some kind of cooking to be done – sometimes pies, often cakes. They nearly always end in pies and or cream being splattered on faces, and often ovens or pies exploding. In this extract Tommy the Cat offers to help Sarah the Cook:

SARAH: So now I'm going to have to bake the pies all by myself.

TOMMY: Well, no – I can help you.

SARAH: You? You haven't got opposable thumbs...

TOMMY: Well me and (POINTING TO AUDIENCE) the other cats in the shop – Wotcha cats!

SARAH: Well, beggars can't be choosers... but all that fur is against health and safety. You need an overall.

TOMMY: An overall what?

SARAH: Here, you can wear this old frock of mine. (SHE HELPS HIM INTO THE DRESS.)

Tommy: So you make the pies in the shop do you?

SARAH: Oh yes.

TOMMY: Doesn't that get in the way?

SARAH: Oh no. There's never any mess. (THEY GIVE THE AUDIENCE A 'LOOK'.)

Once the idea of cooking has been established, instructions can be given and misheard. Flour, water, eggs, etc. can be played with, and thrown about inappropriately. Often, during this, a second bowl is substituted, and the cook miraculously has some finished dough. This is sometimes actual dough (made fresh for every performance), or it can be a form of modelling clay, depending on what you want to do with the dough. It is always good to get stage management to research and test the dough during rehearsals.

TOMMY: Do you knead the dough?

SARAH: Of course I need the dough! I don't work here for free!

TOMMY: NO, I mean do you K-nead the dough?

SARAH: Ah yes! That is what we do next. Would you like to K-nead the dough?

TOMMY: I'd be honoured. (He gets up on the table and uses his knees to knead the dough.)

Tommy the Cat kneading the dough in the slosh scene (actors: Dale Superville and Howard Coggins).

49

SARAH: What are you doing?

TOMMY: I'm K-neading the dough with my K-nees!

SARAH: Oh stop mucking about! Now season it.

TOMMY: (TOMMY SNEEZES RIGHT OVER THE PIE.) Aachoo!

SARAH: What are you doing?

TOMMY: You told me to sneeze on it!

SARAH: No! Season it!

Sometimes the kneading process ends with the dame and the comic character pulling and stretching it, often resulting in the comic character wearing it as a scarf (this will need a specially made dough with more elastic properties). Or, the dough can be placed loosely over a dish. Then beneath the table a hidden crew member pushes a balloon up under it, so that it looks as if the pie is baking or the bread is rising; at an appropriate moment the balloon can then be popped, covering the dame in flour.

Sometimes the dough is plopped in the pie dish (never carefully) and then 'baked' in an oven. The characters then normally get distracted, smoke pours out of the oven and then it explodes, hopefully covering the pair in black dust.

The telephone

This comes from an old Music Hall gag, and needs an old-fashioned early-twentieth-century telephone, with the main body of the phone mounted on a wall. The basic premise is that the person using the phone is calling down for supplies, usually water or flour, and they get these squirted at them through the phone itself. It works better if two people use the phone. One uses it and doesn't get squirted and the other does. It can be inserted into most cooking scenes. Here is a modern variation on the old theme:

SARAH: Now, can you use the phone to call down for some water.

TOMMY: (HE GOES OVER TO 'TELEPHONE TUBE' ON WALL.) Can you send up some water?
(WATER SHOOTS OUT OF THE PHONE AND SQUIRTS TOMMY IN THE FACE, AND DROPS INTO THE BOWL. HE WALKS BACK OVER AND SHOWS HER THE WATER IN THE BOWL.)

SARAH: Can I have a touch more please?

TOMMY: No! It just squirted me.

SARAH: Did it? Did you say please?

TOMMY: Erm...

SARAH: Manners cost nothing. Ask again. Please. (TOMMY LOOKS DUBIOUS BUT WALKS OVER AND SPEAKS INTO THE TUBE AGAIN.)

TOMMY: Can I have some more water – (IT HAPPENS AGAIN) – please? (IT HAPPENS AGAIN. HE IS VERY WET.)

SARAH: Lovely. Isn't cooking fun? Now I need a little flour.

TOMMY: (GIVES HER A FLOWER.) Is this little enough for you?

SARAH: Not Flower. Flour. Floooor. Can you call down for some?

TOMMY: Now, hang on! When I called down for the water it squirted me in the face, what happens if it happens to happen again?

SARAH: You obviously didn't do it properly. You say, 'Please, could you send up some flour?' and move out of the way.

TOMMY: OK, I'll try it. (GOES OVER TO PIPE.) 'Please can I have some flour and move out of the way!' (HE GETS SQUIRTED WITH FLOUR WHICH STICKS TO HIS WET FACE.)

SARAH: Have you seen a ghost? Or are you feeling a bit bucket?

TOMMY: Feeling a bit bucket?

SARAH: Yes, you look a little pail! (MORE COOKING NONSENSE OCCURS – UNTIL ...)

SARAH: Now we need some Pure Fruit

Purée for the Pure Fruit Pie.

TOMMY: Pure Fruit Purée for the Pure Fruit Pie?

Sarah: Yes. Pure Fruit Purée for the Pure Fruit Pie.

TOMMY: And where do we get the Pure Fruit Purée for the Pure Fruit Pie?

SARAH: You'll have to call down for some.

TOMMY: Oh no. I remember the water and the flour. I'm not doing that again.

Sarah: Look, it's easy. Step aside. (SHE GOES OVER TO THE PIPE.) Please could I have some pure fruit purée for the pure fruit pie? (SHE STANDS OUT OF THE WAY AND POINTS THE TUBE DOWN INTO THE DISH. A SMALL AMOUNT OF RUNNY FRUIT STUFF COMES OUT.) See? Easy. Now you try.

TOMMY: Please could I have some pure fruit purée for the pure fruit pie? (HE MOVES OUT OF THE WAY – NOTHING HAPPENS.) I said, please could I have some pure fruit purée for the pure fruit pie? (HE STANDS OUT OF THE WAY – NOTHING HAPPENS.) I SAID – PLEASE COULD I HAVE SOME PURE FRUIT PURÉE FOR THE PURE FRUIT – (He gets gunged) – PIE.

One of the benefits of using the telephone as the main component of your slosh scene is that nearly all the mess happens in one spot – right by the phone – so the clear-up afterwards isn't quite so time consuming.

Sitting on the pie

In this gag a pie or cake has been prepared, usually by the dame, to celebrate a moment in the story, or simply cheer everybody up. If it's a cake, it is best made from foam rubber that can be covered in creamy gunge. This means it is soft and re-useable night after night. If it's a pie, a firmer but still soft substance needs to be used for the pie base, such as Plastazote foam, and lashings of gungey cream smeared on top. They need to be large and very visible. Whether it's a cake or pie, the audience needs to guess, as soon as they see it, that someone is going to end up messy....

Often it is the comic character who orchestrates this business. They want someone (often the dame

Dale Superville, as Tommy the Cat, getting gunged in the mouth. The telephone had three separate plastic tubes (one for each of the substances squirted). Squeezy bottles secured to the ends of the tubes offstage were operated by a crew member on cue.

or the baddie) to sit on the pie. They need to place the pie behind the intended recipient and try and get them to sit down. Each time the recipient needs to nearly sit, but change their minds at the last minute (usually three times, preferably in three different places). The pie then needs to be removed from the hands of the comic character and placed on a different chair, and then without remembering, the comic character gets their come-uppance by sitting down on the pie and getting their own bottom covered in gunge. You can also (or instead) move the pie to the table and somehow the comic character gets their face pushed into the cake.

Getting ready and make-up

A scene which sometimes crops up in *Cinderella* has the Ugly Sisters getting ready to go to the ball, and is usually staged in a dressing-room or bathroom. It might have them getting washed in a shower that pours 'cold' water on an unsuspecting swim-suited sister, or it can be the make-up and potions that they apply to their face in order to beautify themselves for the Prince.

This slosh scene is different because the recipient wants it to happen. To get the most enjoyment from this scene, the script needs to itemize the comical ingredients in the gunge, so that the audience, and not the gungee, know what is in it (sprouts, smelly socks, bogies, etc.). The scene is orchestrated so that the beauty products described (by Buttons) sound good – the newest moisturizer 'to make you look ten years younger', a potion to make the hair gleam, etc. Then these potions can be offered up and begged for by the Ugly Sisters.

```
BUTTONS:   But I can't let you have this
           super-soft cream! This Oil of
           (DOES SPANISH DANCE) Olé!
UGLY 1:    Why not?
BUTTONS:   This has been specially made
```

Silly Billy sniggering as he tries to entice the snooty Mayor to sit down on the cake in Jack and the Beanstalk *(actors: Christopher Robert, Andrea Miller and Dale Superville; lighting design by John Harris).*

```
                for (Celebrity name)!
UGLY 2:     Ooh!
BUTTONS:    Without this, her face falls
            off.
UGLY 1:     I don't care! Give it to me!!!
BUTTONS:    You want me to give it to you?
UGLY 1:     Yes! Give it to me!
BUTTONS:    (Takes out an enormous
            handful of bright blue
            cream.) Shall I give it to
            her, boys and girls? I
            shouldn't, should I?...
            Should I?
UGLY 2:     Give it to me!
BUTTONS:    Right then, here it is! (HE
            SPLODGES THE CREAM ALL OVER
            UGLY 1'S FACE). Ooh. You look
            better already.
UGLY 1:     Mmm! Tastes nice too.
```

In Joe Graham's script of *Cinderella*, not only did the 'Uglies' ask for all this gunk to be put on them, it then dyed their faces, so that they were stained with blue and orange for the Ball.

Gunge tank

Modern pantomimes sometimes have a 'gunge tank' similar to those used on some children's game-shows, which can be great, if a suitably silly reason can be shoe-horned into the story – perhaps one of the characters is a mad inventor? Or it's a new self-tanning booth?

The gunge is held within a sealed container, similar to a shower cubicle, which whoever is being 'gunged' has to get into. This person is often the comic character, or occasionally the 'baddie'. The script needs to create some reason why they would get in there in the first place. If it's a baddie, then it's often their vanity or evilness that has led them there, whilst the comic character could be easily fooled into entering it. The person operating the tank is often the dame, or can be the comic

Dale Superville and Kieran Buckeridge as the Ugly Sisters receiving their 'beauty treatments' courtesy of Daniel Crowder's Buttons in Cinderella *(script by Joe Graham; lighting design by John Harris).*

character if it's the baddie being 'gunged'.

Don't have the baddie operating the gunge tank, because the audience will want to see the gunging happen, but if the baddie is in charge, they will feel torn as to which side they are on! You can of course have the baddie in charge if his/her evil plans go wrong, and in order to show how the gunge tank works they climb in it themselves and end up getting 'gunged'! Tanks that work every time and don't get their pipes clogged can be difficult to build, and will need testing during rehearsals. You don't want to set up the big moment and then only a dribble of goo to come out.

The other type of gunge tank is more like a small pool, and the person being gunged has to jump, or is pushed into it from a height. This is more fail-safe in operation, but you need a deep enough pool so that the actor isn't going to hurt themselves by jumping in. A pool of that size will need careful storage and consideration as to how it is to be manoeuvred into position, and its weight in relation to the tolerance of the stage floor.

Gunge tank scenes can involve a quiz show element: the person being gunged is asked a series of questions; if they fail to answer correctly, they get 'gunged'. The questions can either be impossibly hard so that there is no way of avoiding the mess, or very easy – but the 'gungee' is too silly to know the answers even if the audience are calling them out. The questions can also be a simple children's joke:

```
DAME:        Now, everyone knows this:
             what's black and white and
             red all over?
SILLY
BILLY:       Erm... What's black and white
             and red all over? Oh, I know
             this! It's a newspaper!
DAME:        No! I'm afraid not. What's
             black and white and red all
             over? An embarrassed penguin.
             Aw. What a shame. (SHE PULLS
             THE LEVER AND HE IS GUNGED.)
```

Wallpaper scene

A wallpapering scene can go down extremely well,

harking back to memories of Laurel and Hardy films. It involves lots of 'paint' (normally a very watered-down solution), lots of wallpaper paste going everywhere and wallpaper stood on and stuck in the wrong places. Again it is often led by the dame, with the comic character becoming their assistant, but can work well if you have an alternative double-act in the story. Within this set piece, at some point some, most, or all of the following will happen:

- A bucket of paste is placed somewhere (normally the foot of a ladder) and someone accidentally steps in it. They cannot get the bucket off and walk around with it stuck to their foot.
- A bucket of paint is filled, but it has no bottom, and the person holding the bucket gets paint all over their feet.
- A bucket of paint is filled, but there is a small hole in it and so the paint spurts out. As someone climbs a ladder the spurting paint goes all over their partner.
- One person tries to straighten out a roll of wallpaper on a pasting table in order to paste it. They eventually get it flat, but then have to let go in order to get a pasted brush and the roll recoils. This happens three times. In trying to flatten out the paper, the 'paster' tries various physical positions, often nearly lying on the paper, but then realizes they can't reach the paste brush. Eventually, both characters straighten out the wallpaper, and one holds as the other starts to paste. This always ends up with the one holding the paper getting 'pasted' by the other. It might be just their hand or arm, or if the comic character has managed to get themselves into a daft position with their head on the table to keep the paper flat, it can even be their face. The 'paster' only notices (often with a double take) once lots of paste has been accidentally applied.
- One character takes the pasted paper and holding it up walks over to a ladder and begins to climb. With each step, they put their foot through the paper onto the ladder rungs, so that by the time they're at the top, they've only

got hold of a tiny bit of paper, which they still endeavour to stick to the wall.

- At any point (or several) one character may get annoyed at being covered in paste/paint and chase the other around the stage.
- The scene often ends with escalating retaliation – a speck of paint on a shirt is retaliated for by pouring paint into the other's top and then splatting it up into their face. A splash of paste in the face may lead to a bucket of paste being tipped over the head or down the trousers.

Whatever happens, the scene always ends in chaos, and often in the final moment a bucket (which the audience thinks is filled with paste or water but has actually been swapped for one with tinsel) is held by the dame who threatens to throw it over the audience and finally does – there is a blackout and the audience scream with delight!

Plate scene

The mess in this 'slosh' scene is created by plates being dropped and smashed. In this scenario the dame wants washed plates put away, and the comic character is trying to help, but getting it all wrong. Often this involves a double 'plate-slide' contraption (a narrative reason, however silly, for having this is needed). The plates are slowly slid down alternate slides and caught for the first few attempts, but then the sliding goes wrong, the audience can see the plates coming but often the actors get distracted or just can't cope, and so the catching goes wrong till they are left with a huge pile of broken crockery. This is successful because the audience knows what's going to happen and are party to the gag by shouting out which slide to go to, or calling for the plates. The more confusing and noisy, the more the children love it.

With the plate scene you need to consider several things. Firstly, health and safety: it can only

The aftermath of the plate scene in Mother Goose *at Oldham Coliseum showing the paired plate slides (Fine-Time Fontayne as Mother Goose; design by Celia Perkins; photography by Ian Tilton).*

work where there is some distance between the audience and the stage effect, as when the plates shatter the pieces can cover large distances. Secondly, the cost of buying plates that shatter easily (biscuit-fired unglazed plates obtained directly from a pottery) can be prohibitive as large quantities are required for each performance to make it funny.

The design and construction of the slides needs to be big enough to get the right effect, which may cause storage issues in the wings. They also need to be the right length and set at the right angle for the joke to work, so you may need to test this out with a plank of wood and plates, checking for the appropriate angle/speed before going on to build the chutes. There's no point going to all the trouble and expense for the plates not to slide at the right speed for the joke.

OTHER TRADITIONAL SET PIECES

Ghost scene

This is also known as the 'behind-you' scene, and is an essential element in any pantomime. The audience, young and old, enjoy shouting out the phrase, 'It's behind you', and as pantomime storylines often deal with tales of travel and bravery, there's normally somewhere that a moment like this can work.

This scene normally involves the dame, the comic character, and the hero and/or heroine. The main characters are normally somewhere new to them, either the Giant's castle, Abanazar's Palace, or somewhere creepy, like a forest at night. Ideally, the situation, and the 'ghost' fit in with the storyline.

Whatever the situation, the characters admit to being a bit scared:

```
SILLY
BILLY:      This place gives me the
            creeps!
JILL:       They say that this forest is
            full of ghosties and
            ghoulies!
DAME:       I don't want to be grabbed by
```

the ghosties!
```
SILLY
BILLY:      And I don't want to be grabbed
            by the... ghosties either!
```

Someone suggests that they sing a song to banish their fears. The audience is then asked to shout out if they see a ghost. Our heroes then begin to sing the song. The 'ghost' then appears upstage of the main characters. When the audience shouts, our heroes can't hear, and so have to ask the audience to repeat themselves. Once they have established that there is a 'ghost' in the vicinity they have to ask the audience where it is. The audience of course replies, 'It's behind you!' By the time our heroes understand and look, the ghost has gone (or hides), and so they continue the song. This is repeated, but the ghost gets braver and scares first the heroine, who runs off, and then the comic character, who also runs off. Finally the dame is left singing the song on her own and when the ghost creeps up on her and they turn to face each other ... after a pause, it is the ghost who screams and runs off! There are lots of variations on this, and you must tailor the scene to fit your story.

In a version of *Dick Whittington* at Hackney Empire the heroes found themselves in a jungle, and the 'ghost' was an enormous gorilla – it looked big enough to be daunting, but had a comic touch to its design so that the younger children weren't too scared. In a similar place in the story of *Dick Whittington* at Watford Palace Theatre, our heroes found themselves in an underwater kingdom and were chased by a very smiley octopus, which was inhabited by three people!

Mirror scene

This is based on an old Music Hall and Vaudeville act, and is rarely used in modern pantomimes, but it can be brilliant. It involves a very large frame, which should resemble a mirror. Someone, usually the dame, is looking into the mirror and seeing herself. But the 'reflection' is played by another actor in exactly the same costume behind the frame.

The gist of it is that as the dame looks into the mirror and moves, the reflection reacts and moves

gauzed section for
seeing out of

gauzed eyes.

Octopus from Dick Whittington and his Cat, *which had three performers providing six of the legs (pictured with the Dame, played by Howard Coggins).*

just as a reflection ought to – but not quite. The dame becomes suspicious, and tries 'testing' the reflection with increasingly more and more complicated moves, and quick double takes, until she is satisfied that it is a true reflection. At this point the reflection then does something completely different and silly and is found out, and so the scene ends with the dame running after the culprit, often through the mirror.

The reason the scene is rarely done is it doesn't really add to the story as such, and yet requires a lot of rehearsal time to get right. However, if it is done well it can be one of the highlights of the evening. For reference look at film and television versions, such as the Marx Brothers' iconic mirror scene and Dawn French and Darcy Bussell's more modern take of it in *The Vicar of Dibley*.

Money scene

Many pantomime stories have the dame and the comic character experiencing some financial difficulties. There is often some rent to be paid, or someone in need of a little extra cash, and at these moments often a money gag of some sort is used. They can take various forms:

Looking for lost money

Someone comes on stage to sing a song. The dame and comic character then come on claiming to have lost a pound. They search everywhere, frisking the singer, going into the audience, etc. and eventually give up and go off just as the song is coming to an end. The singer then lifts their foot, reveals the coin and puts it in their pocket.

Paying the rent

The dame is asked for the rent and borrows the money from the person she owes it to. She then offers to pay them back. When paying them she counts out the money, stopping every now and then to ask a series of questions which have numerical answers:

DAME: OK, here's your money. One, two, three… how many brothers did you say you had?

MAN: Six.

DAME: Six? (CONTINUES TO COUNT OUT MONEY.) Seven, eight, nine… and what age were you when you got married?

MAN: Twenty-one.

DAME: ... twenty-two, twenty-three, twenty-four... and how long have you been married now?

MAN: Forty years!

DAME: Forty? Forty-one, forty-two… And so on.

There are also many money games, which seem easy when explained, but there is often a hidden and misleading point that the dame hasn't mentioned:

DAME: I bet you five pounds that I can get you to say the word 'yes'.

COMIC: No! You won't be able to. I'll accept the bet!

DAME: Are you ready?

COMIC: Yes.

DAME: I win!

The trick gets more convoluted as it continues, but always ends up with the comic character losing quite a lot of money. Often these 'tricks' are then passed on from one character to another, with the Comic then trying the trick out on the next person. This often doesn't work out, and the comic character, though in charge of the game, still loses. These 'tricks' can work well, and you can often see younger members of the audience trying them out on their relatives after the performance. For an in-depth study of different money gags and other such pantomime tricks read *The Pantomime Book* by Paul Harris, an excellent source of all the traditional gags (*see* Further Reading).

Songsheet

This is where one of the central characters, usually the comic character or the dame (or both), teach the audience a song. It is usually sited just prior to the finale, because putting it there allows time for a major scene change (the finale being set upstage of the frontcloth). It will also allow all except the two characters leading it time to change into their finale costumes, meaning that only these two characters will require a quick change.

The song itself can either be a traditional catchy song that most of the children will know, or a variation with lyrics adjusted to fit the particular story, or it can even be a completely new song. Whichever, it needs to lend itself to having lots of physical actions, that everyone can learn quickly, and be easily repeatable. Often, once the audience has had a few goes at the song, some pre-selected children are invited up onto the stage. Ideally this selection should be done by the Front of House Manager during the interval. They can spot lively children, children with birthdays, or indeed quieter children who may get a real thrill from getting up on stage.

Never get children up on stage who don't want to be there! It's a terrible experience for them, and the rest of the audience will be made to feel uncomfortable. A good number is four children, and aged four to eight. Younger than that and they can have difficulties speaking, and older children

can get embarrassed. Once they are on stage the actors ask them questions about their ages, perhaps what presents they are hoping to get/have got for Christmas, and perhaps something about the show so far – 'What was your favourite bit?' Often there is one child who seems the most verbal/cute/funny who is usually placed at the end of the line. Then they all get to sing the song through with the characters on stage and with the audience helping out.

After an enormous round of applause, goody bags are handed out. This might be a bag of sweets from a local sponsor, a reminder of the show, or a balloon – just a 'something' to reward the children for their hard work. Each child gets a goody bag, except the last child. The dame or comic character need to look as if they've forgotten the child until it is brought to their attention either by the child or the audience. This child is then invited to do the song again – but with some variation. They might need to wear a silly costume/hat, they might have to do it at double speed, or they might have to conduct the audience. Once they have had their moment of fame, they get a huge round of

Dale Superville as Tommy the Cat leading the songsheet in Dick Whittington and his Cat.

applause and are handed their goody bag.

When bringing children on stage you do need to make sure that your actors are great with kids and can ad lib easily, as what the children say is really unpredictable, and you need actors who are adept at keeping everything moving. They must be able to react well to the direction a particular child might take a conversation. If this combination is right, these moments can be priceless.

Another variation on the songsheet is to get a competition going in the auditorium. Either two different songs with similar beats, or the same song with different lyrics can be used. This is normally led by two characters. The song or songs are taught and then the characters on stage decide that their song/version is better and that they should have a competition. They divide the auditorium in half and both songs are sung so that the loudest side wins, this is normally decided by the musical director in the pit, who often declares it a draw!

Ideally at the end of this scene the audience should be left to do the song(s) through one more time as our characters dash off to get changed for the finale. Sometimes this can be conducted by your audience stooge!

In our production of *Aladdin* at Watford Palace Theatre, the songsheet song was an adaptation of the popular children's song 'Heads, Shoulders, Knees and Toes' but changed, by Wishee Washee, because of the laundry theme of the show, into 'Hats, Jackets, Socks and Pants'. The lyrics were painted onto a large pair of Y-fronts, and the actions of the song pointed to the various items of clothing. The song proved such a hit that the following year, at one performance, when Dick Whittington's Cat said, 'We're going to sing a song! Now which song shall we sing?' a young member of the audience shouted out, 'Hats, Jackets, Socks and Pants!'

Birthdays and shout-outs

'The birthdays' is when one of the characters, usually the dame or the comic character, reads out a list of people who have attended that particular performance. It may be a local scout group, a school, an office group, or someone with a birthday.

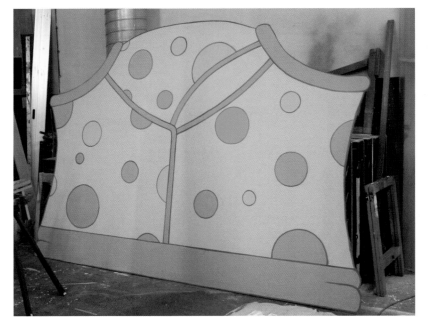

The 'pants' songsheet designed for **Aladdin**, *before the words were added.*

The list is usually compiled during the interval by the Front of House Manager, who will have prior knowledge of large groups or school bookings, and can spot people with birthday badges on. Often people ask, 'Who do I speak to about getting a mention?' This list is then handed to the appropriate actor at the end of the interval.

This moment can happen almost anywhere in the second half, and is usually a frontcloth scene, while the set is being changed behind. Often it occurs just before the songsheet.

The characters read out the names and ask for a shout back. Some people can be quite shy, so having to shout out something silly actually makes it easier. So saying, 'If I call your name out can you shout out, as loudly as you can – Brussels Sprouts!' can work better than just asking for a cheer. It is good for your actor leading this to have some pre-prepared 'lines', such as a joke about being a Brownie, or a comment about the different areas that people come from – 'Oooh, that's the posh end!'

The general shout-outs are done first, then the birthdays – with ages. If you get a particularly young birthday the actor can usually get an 'ah!' from the audience and if it's an older audience member, some gentle joke about their age often goes down well. A standard joke to use (also handy in case there aren't any birthdays) is:

DAME: Oh, and Ladies and Gentlemen, boys and girls, we have a very special birthday here

tonight. Oh yes. Gladys Omeroyd from Rochdale is here tonight celebrating her birthday, and today she is a hundred and eleven! I think that deserves a round of applause, don't you? (APPLAUSE.) Where is she? Where are you Gladys? (PRETENDS TO GET SOME INSTRUCTIONS FROM SOMEONE IN THE WING, AND RE-READS HIS NOTES.) What do you mean, she's not 111? It says here... Oh, no, hang on a minute. She's not 111, no. She's ill.... Oh. Well sorry about that. Get well soon Gladys. Anyway… (SCRUNCHING NOTES INTO A BALL AND THROWING IT INTO THE PIT), shall we sing Happy Birthday to all the other people? Right then, one, two, three!

When the song gets to the part where the person's name is mentioned your actor leading the song can either say 'Happy Birthday to... Everyone!' Or, if they have a great memory they can try and point at the birthday girls and boys around the auditorium saying the names very quickly – 'Happy Birthday dear Chloe, Sally, James, Scott and Michael!' – which can be very impressive.

5 DESIGN OF THE OPEN STAGE

Having now looked at the traditions, structuring and pantomime's set pieces it is time to begin developing the design of the space that all this will happen in. It is important to first develop what is called the 'open stage' as soon as the scene outline for the script has been created, as consideration of the open stage space will help establish the visual and scripted world of your chosen pantomime. This is where the close collaboration between the writer and the designer can reap great rewards.

Before beginning the design process it is important to understand that you should not attempt to reinvent the genre. The style of pantomime has been established for many years, and the look is as much a tradition as the action. Audiences expect to see the cartoon-like painted sets which marry so well with the storytelling and performance formats.

WHY CREATE THE DESIGN FOR THE OPEN STAGE FIRST?

The open stage refers to the design of the empty theatre space and its portals and the floor, which together create the framing for your pantomime. It

The 'open stage' as designed for **Dick Whittington and his Cat.**

is important to emphasize how the creative and practical decisions made for the open stage will impact on the overall creation of the final pantomime.

Considering the venue and acting space of your production at the start of the process will create a pantomime in sympathy with the building's features and available space. It is very easy to get carried away with all the tricks and scenery

OPPOSITE: *The 1:25 scale model from* **Cinderella** *showing the two different sets of portals for the enchanted forest/Hardup Hall scenes and the Royal Palace.*

necessary to create the locations and story, and not consider how these fit within the space available.

It is important to see the 'open stage' as an integral part of the design and not just about masking the offstage areas. The design of this aspect will set the style for the rest of the production. Remember that pantomime is much more likely to play to full houses, which means that the extreme sightline seats are likely to be filled and their view of the stage will include a lot of the side of stage. Taking the design right off into the wings will therefore complete the stage 'picture' for them.

Another reason for designing the open stage first is to allow the opportunity for the construction and painting of the set to be split into more than one build period. Some regional theatres have to begin work on the construction of the sets well in advance of the production. This could even be as early as late spring before its Christmas opening.

Pantomime is often their biggest production of the year and it is usually impossible to build it all within the period leading up to the production. If they have an in-house workshop, they will inevitably have other commitments within the theatre's autumn season. Having the portals and floor fully designed and ready for construction and scenic painting allows this aspect of the set to be built first. However, at least a rough design/format of the rest of the show will need to be completed alongside the finished design of the portals and floor (for costing purposes). This will need to be done before theatres will give the financial go-ahead for any construction. The design of the rest of the set will be discussed in more detail in Chapter 8.

By giving the construction team this initial part of the set to build, the creative team will also have

Design sketch for Cinderella *showing the design of the portal with its scroll-work and indication of fibre optic lights (Ian Westbrook and 3D Creations production for Bradford Alhambra).*

more time to tweak the script and design for the rest of the show.

In large-scale commercial pantomime the design of the open stage is also of paramount importance. Ian Westbrook, when talking about his design of *Cinderella* for Qdos Entertainment states, 'All the Portals were drawn as scrolled etchings and I wanted them backed with black serge with colour-changing fibre optics inserted into them. In the five portals we put nearly seven miles of fibre optics which took four people six weeks to glue in and fix. All this effort was worth it because when it was lit everything was a complete star field of twinkling lights.' Portals are explained and discussed in more detail later in this chapter.

GETTING READY FOR A SITE VISIT

Before beginning to develop the script and the design, it is essential that you take the opportunity to review what the space/stage has to offer. The creative team should arrange a site visit, as the theatre plans will give the dimensions but not the quality and atmosphere that the space has, and some of its architectural attributes are only evident when you see them in reality.

Prior to this visit, it is good to meet up and discuss a scene outline for the pantomime. This only needs to be the briefest of descriptions about the action and the order in which the scenes might take place, but having this will enable a closer and more fruitful examination of the staging implications and possibilities.

Smaller-scale and non-conventional theatre spaces

In most instances a pantomime will have a designated theatre stage. On very small-scale productions, for example in community halls, you may have to build your stage from blocks or steel deck and create a proscenium arch (the open-framed wall dividing the acting area from the auditorium). This can be a huge task but it also offers the opportunity to establish the size and style of the space to meet with your specific pantomime ideas. However, it will also mean that you are going to be limited in what you can do in the way of transformation between scenes, as storage and access might be limited and there will be no possibility of flying set pieces. You are also going to have to be creative with your lighting and sound as it may need bringing into the venue. Work with the simplicity and consider making sound acoustically, and with lighting, think about a general cover with the odd 'special' (for example a specific light and colour for the entrance of your baddie). This limited resource is a great opportunity to use hand-held lights such as torches and lanterns as part of the concept of your pantomime.

In venues without an inbuilt theatre stage, you may want to consider other staging options that do away with the need for a proscenium arch. By staging a production 'in the round' or in a thrust style ('thrust' is where the stage projects out into the space with the audience on three sides surrounding it), some aspects of traditional pantomime can be quite a challenge (absence of frontcloth, the action of 'behind-you' moments), but these staging styles do offer a closer relationship with the audience, and for a family audience this added 'contact' can be a real thrill and can intensify their experience. However, these decisions need to be made early so that you can tailor your script, design and production accordingly.

Working with the possibilities of the space

In larger venues you might have an established stage at one end of the room with a raised stage and front tabs on a simple tab track. Here you might also have a small lighting rig and basic sound system to work with. Again space might be an issue due to the lack of offstage area and lack of flying facilities. However, clever use of cloths on 'rollers', and 'legs' that are on turntables, can mean that you can go some way to doing some scene changes within your pantomime. It is always important with venues where you have some, but limited, theatrical resources, not to over-complicate the design. It is very easy to make things too big and cumbersome and limit the acting space and slow down the pace of the show. Keep your concept simple and bold. Look for the essentials of the story and work on creating those

Big Top pantomime

An example of an alternative venue being used for pantomime is *Robinson Crusoe* by the company of the Theatre Royal, Bury St Edmunds.

Whilst the Theatre Royal was being renovated for two years the pantomime had to be housed outside of the Theatre. A Big Top was selected for this so it could still happen locally. The 'Big Top' we used was the tent that the National Theatre had built (originally for their tour of *Oh! What A Lovely War*), so it was purpose-built as a theatre space, with a dark-coloured lining so that you could lose the walls under show lighting.

The audience was seated in-the-round with one fifth of the circle removed to house the set. This was an island mountain with huts and palm trees etc., which could house the band and also provide a set that could be climbed up and swung down from during the show. It could also be adapted for different locations around the island.

Robinson Crusoe was very well suited to the space as this story, unlike a lot of pantomime stories, could be told entirely on the island. Being a 'Big Top' also meant that some of the performers cast in the show were acrobats who could do spectacular trapeze and aerial work, making full use of the venue's possibilities.

It was also quite nice because it was a tent and fully heated – it gave a really tropical atmosphere that contrasted well with the cold mid-winter weather outside.

Will Hargreaves: set and costume designer

The model, the finished space and the outside for the 'Big Top' version of Robinson Crusoe *at Bury St Edmunds (design by Will Hargreaves; photography by Keith Mindham).*

moments well, rather than all the different locations. Again these issues need to be considered right at the beginning of the project – when the story is first being discussed. Then a script could be written with fewer locations, in order to keep the design and staging simpler.

Sound considerations

In a smaller venue, it is unlikely that your performers will be amplified and your music might be recorded or played acoustically so again consider how this is going to work. During the site visit it is good to test this out. If you are using recorded music you may want to think about the placement of speakers – both aesthetically and acoustically. How much echo and bounce is there in the space? How much are the performers going to have to project their voices? Bear in mind when doing this that once you have the audience in the auditorium, and the stage dressed, the sound

quality will change, as some sound will be absorbed and some will bounce back.

If the music in the show is to be played live, consider where your musicians might be located – are they going to be on stage as part of the action? Is there an orchestra pit or area somewhere to the side or back? Some venues have a balcony area which can be perfect for musicians – or perhaps a raised area can be created on stage. If the musicians are going to be very visible, there may be a way of tying in the 'band' area to the design as a whole.

Also, whilst in the venue, check how much of a blackout can be achieved. Are you going to have to supply your own black drapes to put up against windows to create this? Remember with pantomime you are inevitably going to do matinées, so preventing daylight from leaking into the space is going to be important.

The upper circle view (model) showing how upstage more than half of the height is obscured, and how the design of the portal allows best possible viewing upstage centre for **Aladdin.**

THE TRADITIONAL PROSCENIUM STAGE

When working in a proscenium theatre, look carefully at what the stage can offer. Begin by looking at the auditorium from the stage itself. It is important to gauge what the performers will see of their audience, as so much of pantomime is about the contact and asides that characters make with the audience. Remember that in a lot of cases the band will be placed between the stage and the audience, and in some theatres without a built-in orchestra pit an amount of seating may be removed to accommodate the band. The actual distance between stage and audience may therefore be greater than you think.

It is really important to look at the spatial relationship between actors and audience – including how much distance has to be covered to make that link. In theatre spaces there is what is referred to as a 'sweet spot' – a place on stage, normally central and towards the front, which actors gravitate to. It is invariably the central spot visually, and is often the best area acoustically. The design will need to keep this area free from obstruction and accessible at all times.

If your theatre has boxes, is there quick access from there to the stage – either directly (perhaps by ladder) or via back stairs? These may be interesting entrances or exits. Boxes can sometimes provide an extra unexpected place for a short speech.

Next, move into the auditorium and check the sightlines from the extreme seats on all levels. It is so easy to find that either the very front of the stage, upstage or the top of the proscenium can be obscured from different parts of the audience seating. It is important that you don't create important narrative moments in the pantomime that go unseen. The balcony or upper circle is where this occurs most, and is also where the school parties are quite often housed. They can be some of the best at participation so it is crucial that they can see everything. Remember when checking this to have someone sitting in the seat in front. An adult will block more of the view than the empty seat and some of the audience members in the front rows might lean on the balcony edge

and obscure more of the view.

If you are considering any unusual entrances/exits, chases, or if you are planning to use the boxes, again check the sightlines. Though these can be a brilliant way of surprising an audience and getting younger audiences screaming with delight, it can fall very flat if a large section of the audience cannot see, and therefore feel that they are missing out.

Understanding the limits of the stage visually

The late-Georgian theatre at Bury St Edmunds has two doors either side of the proscenium, which are great assets as they provide ready-made entrances for the spirits of good and evil to use. It also has a forestage which is used extensively in all productions because of the tricky sightlines that exist within this theatre. The auditorium is horseshoe-shaped and the boxes curve around right up to the edge of the proscenium. Because of this shape, you only get an equilateral triangle of space, stretching part way upstage behind the proscenium, which is visible from all seats of the auditorium. This means there is not a great deal of usable acting space on stage. Plus, they remove part of the forestage to get in extra seats and the band. This creates a very tight acting area that is always a challenge.

Will Hargreaves: set and costume designer

View of the stage and its proscenium doors from one of the boxes at the Theatre Royal, Bury St Edmunds (photography by Dennis Gilbert).

Offstage space

Check the wing space and offstage storage areas. It is really important if you have limited or uneven wing space as it will dictate how larger items of set or props access the stage. For example at Watford Palace Theatre there is very little wing space stage right, but wider wing space and storage area stage left so this influenced where our large trucks were positioned on stage. In *Aladdin* we had a Trojan camel in which all the goodies smuggle themselves into Abanazar's Palace. This was so large that it could only be housed in the storage area stage left and then loaded with performers and wheeled on from that side of the stage. This had a knock-on effect on the position of the main seating area for this scene, which then had to be stage right (otherwise it would have obscured the camel when it arrived), and the camel's bulk and position had to be factored in when directing the scene.

If storage in the wings is an issue then you may have to consider storing larger set/prop items upstage of the backcloth and reduce your stage depth.

Also check the clearance height of any of the storage areas as they are quite often lower than the access height from the wings. The space in the wings can also dictate the number of portals that might be required (this will be discussed later in this chapter).

Accessing the stage

Next check the crossover (this is the passage behind the set or theatre wall where actors can cross from one side of the stage to the other). Is there a purpose-built crossover? Is there a corridor behind the back wall? If no corridor exists then you

The Trojan camel with the Genie played by Howard Coggins.

will need to consider bringing your settings far enough downstage to allow for this. The crossover is crucial in pantomime as the speed of entrances and exits is quick and some established pantomime gags rely on a performer exiting one side of stage and appearing from the opposite side, seconds later.

Coming up through the floor

In some theatres there might be traps already built into the stage floor which would give the opportunity to do other interesting entrances and exits. These could be exploring an underworld, such as King Rat's lair in *Dick Whittington*, by

Jack and the Beanstalk *at Theatre Royal, Bury St Edmunds, with the beanstalk positioned in front of the trap so that the characters could appear to climb up through the floor, arriving at the Giant's castle in the clouds (Dennis Herdman as the Dame; design by Will Hargreaves; photography by Keith Mindham).*

having rats crawling up through the stage. Another use might be having the top of the Beanstalk poking through the floor and Jack climbing up to arrive in clouds where the Giant lives. For characters such as the baddie or the Genie in *Aladdin*, a 'grave trap' (where the stage either lowers with the performer on it, or is lowered so that the performer can be placed on it to rise up through the floor) can create surprising or magical entrances especially if accompanied by a pyrotechnic flash or smoke.

Treads

Finally, it is crucial that you have access from the auditorium to the stage via 'treads' (stairs), either centrally or on both sides of the stage. This allows characters access from the stage into the theatre auditorium to interact with the audience. For auditorium chases, check if there is a central aisle, or whether the chase would have to be around the edges of the seating, and also check the access for potential 'run around' sections in the circle and upper circle. It is important to interact with the audience as much as possible. The young audiences get really excited when the action spreads into the auditorium. The treads up and down from the stage are also used when recruiting young audience members to come up onstage for the songsheet, so stair heights should be designed to allow for this.

Variations in the types of proscenium-style theatres

Not all proscenium theatres are alike: some may not have all the facilities, such as a fly-tower (the tower above the stage where the flown scenery is housed when not in use). These theatres may have some limitations, but may have other useful properties when staging pantomime. One such theatre is the Theatre Royal at Bury St Edmunds. This renovated Georgian theatre is run by the National Trust, and has no flying facilities. But being Georgian, it lends itself to the use of sliders and cloths on rollers for creating the different scenes (these will be discussed in more detail in Chapter 8).

DESIGNING THE FLOORS AND PORTALS

The design of the floor and portals establishes the overall look and concept, which will then carry on through to the design of the scenes that fit within it.

Stage floors

Having a well-designed and painted stage floor should never be underestimated in its importance to the overall stage picture. Remember that in the dress circle, upper circle or balcony the audience can see a lot of floor (particularly the upper circle where the floor is the most visible element of the set).

It is best to have the floor designed and painted on sheets of hardboard, a floor cloth, or a dance floor (which can be painted offsite). This will allow more scope for detail and multi-layering of colours. Painting a detailed floor can take hours, as time has to be allowed for colours to dry before applying the next layer. The other option, a 'paint call' (dedicated scenic art time during your technical time or when getting into the space), will not allow enough time for detailed treatments as it has to fit in with the rest of the production/technical schedule and will need a dedicated time slot when the floor is free from other technicians.

If working in a theatre space where the audience is on one level, and this is either flat or only slightly raked, the floor can be less important. But, even here, leaving a floor black will make the design look incomplete. Where possible even a single colour change to match in with the rest of the set will complete the picture.

Designing the floor

The floor is the one aspect of the set which has to work with all the different locations. Sets and cloths can be flown in and out but the floor will remain a constant. Therefore, the way you

Early design stage of the model for Jack and the Beanstalk, *showing how the floor and portals have been considered before the rest of the design and viewed from a height similar to the upper circle.*

The floor for Cinderella was designed to fit with the size of hardboard sheets, so that some of the edges are hidden by the pattern (scenic artist: Aimee Bunyard).

approach the design must reflect this.

For example, in the production of *Cinderella* the scenes include the enchanted forest, inside and outside Hardup Hall, and the Palace. Here different aspects of the floor design related to each location. Within this single floor the green and brown colours represented the enchanted forest, then the tile pattern was designed to work as a slate kitchen floor for Hardup Hall, and the marble effect for the floor to the palace ballroom. With the use of different lighting states, the floor could be made to look very different for each location.

In *Jack and the Beanstalk* the bold crazy-paved design of the floor was a constant, and lit with warm colours through Act 1 for Jack's home town and his Mum's Dairy, which highlighted the pinks and plum colours. Then in Act 2 in Cloudland the strong blues and purples of the paving could be enhanced with blue light to create the effect of being in the clouds.

In *Dick Whittington* the design of the floor was a pantomime version of stage floorboards, but again the use of blue as a background colour meant that the floor could be changed completely when under the sea in Ocean World.

Disguising the wear and tear

One of the factors that can make a pantomime set look tatty is when the floor becomes heavily marked due to the amount of wear and tear. With this in mind it is important to avoid the use of light colours, as these will mark badly and also create bounce for the lighting designer and make it more difficult to isolate characters or moments within the show.

Creating a single-colour floor will show the marks badly. It is best to add a splatter or some sort of painted texture to the surface to break up the flat colour and disguise the marks as and when they happen. Most of the serious marks happen in the get-in and the technical rehearsals. Having a strong glaze applied before it is put down will help avoid some of the wear and tear. A second glaze can be applied to add final protection once the set is up and the floor has been retouched to remove any bad marks.

The best way to disguise marks is to design a patterned stage floor. Heavy patterns and colouring can quite often make quite serious scuffs invisible from the audience's perspective. It can also help disguise the tape marks the crew put

The town square in Jack and the Beanstalk *showing the crazy-paved floor (actors: Dale Superville and Ricardo Coke-Thomas; lighting design by John Harris).*

In Cloudland, using a cooler lighting state brings out different qualities in the flooring (actors: Peter Holdway and Natasha Cox; lighting design by John Harris).

down for positioning trucks and furniture. These tape marks are essential for positioning set and props during the numerous scene changes, so have to be clear enough for the crew to be able to spot quickly in low-level lighting, but they can, within reason, be chosen to be in sympathy with the colours of the floor.

If colours from the floor are to be matched with those of the portals then it is important to understand that using the same colour may not work. The floor and uprights of the portals are on two different planes and when lit the vertical portals will appear darker than the floor. Adjustments need to be made to the shade of the colours to get a closer match.

DRESSING THE FRONT OF THE THEATRE PROSCENIUM

In certain theatres it might be possible to rig a pantomime version of a proscenium arch in front of the usual theatre proscenium. This framing of the stage can really complete the picture that is being created by the onstage design. It is also a good opportunity to include the name of the pantomime. The proscenium can also be fitted with lights, which can either create a night-time of stars when used in conjunction with a onstage 'star cloth'; light-cord and LEDs can also be installed to illuminate the motifs, title or the inside edge of this false proscenium.

If a complete proscenium is not possible then

Original sketch model for Dick Whittington and his Cat *showing the design for a pantomime proscenium.*

Preliminary model for Cinderella *showing a header design that was eventually cut from the final show.*

the design of a 'header', located just behind the proscenium, can be a useful alternative. In most theatres a front header is there to hide the bottom edge of the theatre safety curtain when it is in its 'out' position and/or the downstage lighting bar. It is usually painted black or made of black serge. So replacing this with a designed 'title header' can again add to the overall stage picture.

The first onstage portal can do the same job as a designed false proscenium if necessary. This portal might either be completely different or more complex than the others upstage of it.

PORTALS

Portals are the vertical set pieces that frame the space and the design, and help mask the wings. They are arranged horizontally across the stage, usually diminishing in aperture size the further upstage they go, creating a tunnel-like effect. The closing in creates a false sense of perspective and can make the stage appear much deeper than it is. It also aids the masking of set and props that might be stored in the upstage wing spaces.

A pantomime can have more than one set of portals. If so, one set is usually canvassed flattage and is fixed in position permanently to the stage. The second set, which are fuller than this fixed set, are flown in on flying bars directly in front of the fixed portals. These are usually made as cut cloths (*see* Chapter 8 for definition).

In order to allow the portals to change within the performance, the first fixed portal will remain in constant view to the audience, as the frontcloth that is flown in to cover the subsequent portal changes has to sit directly upstage of it. It should also be remembered that more than one set of portals can create a shortage of free bars for lighting, other cloths, and flown set structures.

Our version of *Cinderella* at Watford Palace Theatre had two sets of portals: a fixed set for the palace and a cut cloth set for the enchanted forest

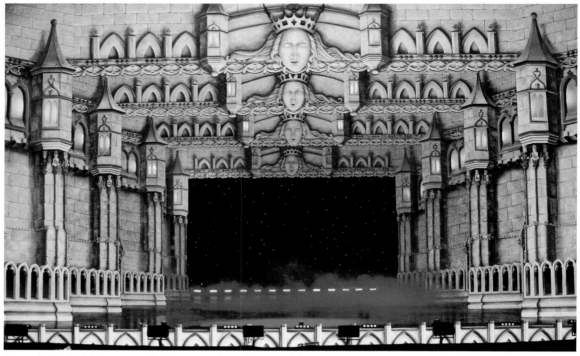

A set of diminishing portals, showing that the use of design and painting can give a sense of false perspective to the turrets and architectural details (**Sleeping Beauty** *design by Ian Westbrook for Qdos Entertainment; lighting design by Ben Cracknell*).

and the scenes set around Hardup Hall. This extra use of bars was accommodated by designing a large truck for Hardup Hall which operated like a dolls' house, opening up to reveal the other rooms required. This meant that there were only four other scenic cloths, so there was still ample room for lighting bars (photographs of this design can seen at the beginning of this chapter and in Chapter 8).

Number of portals

Firstly, the depth of the stage will dictate how many sets of portals are required. The portals are best placed equal distances apart with approximately 1 metre (3ft 3in) between each. This suggestion is an average and might need adjusting if you are bringing large props or set trucks on stage. Larger items are best brought on as far upstage as possible as the issues with sightlines and

therefore width between portals decrease the further upstage you go.

To aid masking the wing space, especially if going wider than 1 metre, you may need to add 'returns' (flattage added at right angles to legs) to the offstage edge. These can be fixed or hinged and angle downstage to help mask the view through to the wings from the extreme seats of the auditorium.

The second aspect to consider is the entrances and exits required within the action of the scenes. However, in most cases it is usual to have a minimum of four portals, the tormentor entrance (discussed below), downstage, midstage and upstage. In a scene that uses the full depth (usually the opening scene and the finale) this will allow for multiple entrances and exits. Remember that if full painted cloths are flown midstage this cuts down on the entrances for those scenes.

The final decision about the position of the

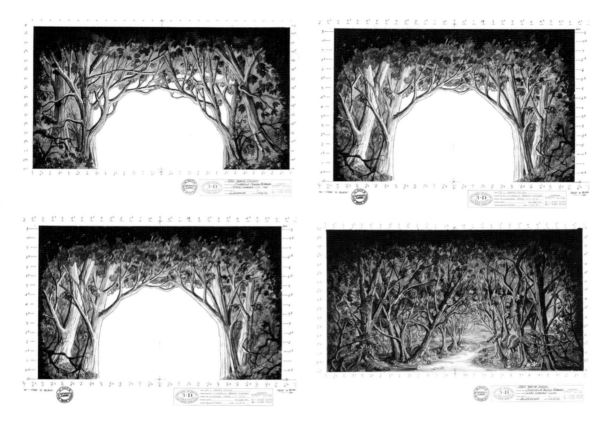

The design and the model for Cinderella *at Bradford Alhambra, showing how three cut-cloth portals together with the clever design of a backcloth can create a great sense of depth and perspective (design by Ian Westbrook).*

Creating portals for multiple use

Commercial pantomimes use their sets for up to ten years, so portals have to be designed to adapt to different-sized venues.

For commercial pantomimes I have developed and designed a series of telescopic portals, one flat upstage of another. So the header sections, and the way they are built, can act almost like a pack of cards that you can slide in and out, so it can expand on the horizontal. Then the legs can go upstage of the header and shutter down, so you can make the portals shorter and smaller when required. Then everything on them has to be designed with that in mind, so you have to allow for this movement in the paintwork and avoid sculptural brickwork or architectural details that would catch. You also have to design them so that if you do shrink them, you don't cut off the tops of turrets etc., which is the hardest thing to calculate.

Ian Westbrook: designer

portals can only be fixed once the sets and all the scenes have been designed, but it is good to have plotted them onto the ground plan first, as priority has to be given to masking the stage space.

Tormentors

Between the theatre proscenium and the first portal on both sides of the stage are the tormentors. 'Tormentors' are the entrances that allow the performers to access downstage of the frontcloth. These are of particular importance for the spirits of Good and Evil to use. The prologue is usually between these two protagonists and often accompanied with pyro flashes, which means the pyrotechnic pods have to be located close to these entrances. (Pyrotechnics will be discussed in more detail in Chapter 10.)

These downstage entrances will be used by other characters throughout the pantomime so tend to be generic in their design. They could match with either the front proscenium, the

Telescopic portals designed and made by Ian Westbrook and 3D Creations for Peter Pan.

The sketch model of Dick Whittington and his Cat. *Here the tormentors were designed to echo the architecture of the theatre boxes.*

Tormentor used as Daisy's stable by folding in a hinged stable door (Dale Superville as Silly Billy and Alice Jackson as the front end of Daisy).

architecture of the auditorium, or the onstage portals.

The stage management prompt desk is usually sited offstage in the wings behind one of the tormentors. So this will have to be taken into consideration as it may block part of one entrance. It is also these entrances where most props are handed on from the wings. As stage management often do this job it is useful that this is close to their prompt desk position in case the deputy stage manger has to perform the task.

Elements of set can be added to the tormentors to give the entrances a different look for specific scenes. For example, in the Trott's Dairy scene in *Jack and the Beanstalk* the tormentor stage right was used for Daisy the Cow's stable. A hinged stable door was simply swung into place for this scene.

Before moving onto the next part of the design
Throughout the development/design of the open stage, dialogue between the writer/director and designer must be ongoing. This will make sure that the content of the script and design marry up and avoid any inconsistencies between the action and the space. It is very easy for either the designer or the writer/director to make presumptions about each other's use of the space, which can carry right through to the rehearsal process where it can often be too late to change. The completion of the open stage will have set the style for the creation of the rest of the production so it is imperative that the creative team shares a common understanding of what this implies.

Sarah the Cook

6 THE CHARACTERS AND THEIR COSTUMES

WHO ARE THE CHARACTERS AND WHY ARE THEY THERE?

When first approaching the characters, you'll need to consider both creative and pragmatic aspects. You need to consider how many performers you'd like in order to tell your story, and then, counter this with how many you might be able to afford or recruit. Also consider the size of your stage: if it's tiny, you might need to limit the performers. In many ways you don't want to bombard your family audience with too many characters, as it can get confusing, but this will need balancing with who is absolutely crucial to tell your story.

There are standard character types that appear in each pantomime, and they all have their various roles within the action of the story. In the well-known stories some of these characters are a given, but if you choose one of the lesser-known plots or are creating a completely new story, you'll still have to consider the archetypal roles required.

Hero or heroine
This should be a central character to sympathize with and relate to. The pantomime is normally their story, and they are often the title character. They are strong and brave and generally good-hearted, though they may make mistakes along the way.

Baddie
Someone who tries to thwart the central character, and who provides the 'conflict' needed to give your storyline some drama. They are normally irredeemably evil, although sometimes they can change at the end with a little magic.

Comic character
This is often the person who has the most interaction with the audience, apart from the dame. They are often friends with or related to the central character. They are usually 'silly' and often get things wrong. Their role is to provide the comedy throughout the piece, and they are often an important part of the hero/heroine's quest.

Magic/good person
These are often in the form of Fairies, but can be more down-to-earth. Their function is to help the central character – either helping them defeat the baddie, or to realize something about themselves (that they have been greedy, naughty, for example). They often speak in rhyme, and are very clear about good and bad.

OPPOSITE: *Costume design for Sarah the Cook in the underwater scene for* Dick Whittington and his Cat.

The above are perhaps the essentials for most stories. However, you will also need to think about the following characters.

Dame

Though not absolutely essential to every plot, a dame would be missed by most pantomime audiences if not included. Sometimes they provide the central role (as in *Mother Goose*), sometimes a mother or nanny figure to the central and/or comic characters, or perhaps paired as the Ugly Sisters. They are the lasting traditional cross-dressed character. They create a direct link with the audience and work well with the comic character to encourage audience participation.

Love interest

Many pantomimes rely on the central character finding their soul-mate, with the finale becoming their wedding. Often the love interest character is the main reason for the quest – if the hero/heroine can become rich, if they can get to the ball, if they can get the treasure for the King, etc., then their chosen one might fall in love with them. Beware of making these characters too 'wet': if they are not interesting enough, the audience might not be that bothered about whether or not the hero/heroine finally gets together with them!

Animal friends/skin parts

A cat, a cow, a goose – there may be an animal already intrinsic to the plot you have chosen. If not, they are often a useful addition to a pantomime story. An animal friend can often become a close confidant of the hero or heroine, which means we get to hear how the central character is really feeling. An animal can also provide story-enhancing frustration, as the animal may have worked out something important (that the baddie is lying/where the jewels are/that the hero is being selfish), but they are often mute, and so unable to directly tell their friend.

Status characters

There are often Kings, Queens or Emperors in the stories, or sometimes Mayors. As the hero/heroine is often poor, these status characters provide a stark contrast with their wealth, and often are part of the family of the intended love interest. The status characters themselves may be a little silly, or a bit pompous, or perhaps both. Sometimes they further the plot by getting into some kind of peril that our hero or heroine needs to fix. Sometimes they become the focus of the dame's romantic aspirational advances.

Comedy sidekicks

These provide a silly foil to a 'straighter' pantomime character. If the baddie has a comedy sidekick (or two in the case of the Broker's Men), this can allow you to reveal the baddie's plans within the dialogue, and also add humour to those scenes – which makes them less terrifying for the younger audience. Sometimes the love interest has a sidekick friend (for instance Prince Charming's servant Dandini), which then balances out the hero/heroine and comic character. Sometimes the status characters have sidekicks (such as Ping and Pong the Emperor's policemen in *Aladdin*), who enable the status character to get things wrong, without looking too silly themselves.

Ping and Pong, the Emperor's police force, played by Joanne Redman and Kieran Buckeridge in Aladdin.

Bo Peep and her magical line-dancing sheep

When writing *Jack and the Beanstalk* I had decided to open with a traditional battle of wills between the goodie and baddie. In Jack, the baddie is usually called Fleshcreep (a great name!), but the fairy's name changes from script to script. I wanted this first encounter to be entirely in rhyme, so I thought it would be great, and make the rhyming easier if I gave the fairy a name that would rhyme with Fleshcreep. There aren't many. I then thought of Bo Peep, which seemed wrong at first – not a fairy's name. Then I thought a family audience would recognize the name, and that plot-wise she could be pretending to be a humble shepherdess, hiding her magical powers, and her sheep could in some way help her perform her magic.

I spoke to Keith, who loved the idea, suggesting gingham fabric for Bo Peep's costume, which then led to her and her sheep having a 'country and western' quality. Keith then suggested that maybe some line-dancing could happen. The choreographer said that she could use line-dancing to choreograph the moment when the fairy casts her spell on the beanstalk, and the musical director then suggested changing a modern rock hit into a country-style yodelling song. Our magic spell scene now had a novel twist, together with humour and magic. And all that from the name!

Joyce Branagh

The junior chorus as Fairy Bo Peep's line-dancing sheep in **Jack and the Beanstalk.**

Chorus

For many stories it is very useful to have a chorus of adults and/or young people who become villagers, magical dancers, baddie's gang, etc.

Getting the balance between male and female

As you put together your cast of characters, look down the list and see what the male/female split is. Are nearly all your actors going to be male? This often happens, as pantomime stories tend to focus more on the male characters. This might not be a problem, but as approximately half your audience are going to be female, you may want to try and address the balance somewhat, for example by changing an Emperor to an Empress, or making the baddie's sidekick female. A more even mix of male and female creates the possibility for everyone to be happily paired up for the finale.

What's in a name?

Some characters will have a designated name that is fixed by the particular pantomime story. But, for those that are open to interpretation, coming up with the appropriate names for characters can be a really good setting off point for the development of the plot lines and costumes. For example the difference between 'Fairy' and 'Fairy Bo Peep' and 'Mayor' and 'Mayor McSpotty' is clear. Bo Peep and McSpotty immediately signify possible directions that the character and costume designs might take.

ANALYSING EACH PANTOMIME CHARACTER IN MORE DETAIL

The rest of this chapter now looks at the considerations that you should make when writing and designing the different traditional characters.

Chorus

Junior chorus

They can help define the historic period. As townspeople, servants and so on, the junior chorus help to identify where we are. It is a good idea to begin the plans for costumes with this chorus, as once the townspeople or servants are established, the decisions about the costuming of the other characters that live in the town or palace can be linked, or deliberately chosen to stand out from the crowd. It is also useful because these costumes have to be made in multiples (shared by two teams of junior chorus on different performance dates). This means costumes are often approximated to ages rather than accurate individual measurements so can be completed early in the making process without individual fittings.

Costuming the junior chorus involves striking the balance between simplicity and detail. Because of the quantity of costumes you don't want to make them too complex, but also it is important that they have as much care and attention to detail as the rest of the company's costumes.

Audiences love seeing the junior chorus dressed as animals, the obvious ones being the mice in *Cinderella*. It is amazing how cute a street-wise child can be when you put him or her in a white fur hood and pink ears.

They might also be creatures in a UV light (ultra-violet) ballet scene. In this case fluorescent fabrics and UV paint can be utilized on top of black leotards to create an interesting array of creatures, particularly for underwater scenes.

Adult (dancing) chorus
Some pantomime producers prefer to use adults instead of (or as well as) the junior chorus, but they will cost more both from the point of view of their wages and the need for more quantity of fabric. However, they will swell the ensemble numbers, both visually and vocally, which can be a big help when trying to balance voices in big musical numbers.

Similar to the junior chorus, they will help define the historic period and are likely to be statuesque, which can add to the level of glamour and spectacle through the use of sumptuous

Costume designs for the junior chorus from Dick Whittington and his Cat.

Costume designs for the adult chorus for the ballroom scene of **Cinderella**
(design by Terry Parsons for First Family Entertainment).

fabrics, feather and jewels for those scenes in a pantomime where the costumes need to impress, such as the ballroom scene or the finale/walk-down.

Hero/principal boy

The hero must have an instant audience appeal. This might be cuteness and wanting to mother him or alternatively because he is dashing and handsome. The character Aladdin has both aspects: he begins as the downtrodden street urchin and ends as a royal prince. His charm should be boyish and when transformed into the prince there should be the sense that he is ill at ease in his clothes. This can be done by making his initial costumes appear really comfortable and

then his princely attire more structured and constricting. As a hero, he is youthful, so it is best to keep his clothes higher on the neck with no chest showing.

Where the hero is a prince from the onset, his appearance should be dashing and stylish throughout. The use of colours with this type of hero should be less comical and more refined, and the fit should accentuate their physique. Where appropriate, colours can be linked to the heroine or love interest. So when they fall headlong in love, they look paired visually as well. However, if their love grows, so should the connection within their clothing.

Jack in *Jack and the Beanstalk* and Dick in *Dick Whittington* join the boyish charm of Aladdin with

85

Oliver Tompsett as Prince Charming finding the glass slipper (pictured with Stephen Boswell as Dandini).

the suaveness of Prince Charming, because with both, there is a sense of them fulfilling their destinies. With Jack it is important that his costume makes a link with his quest to climb the beanstalk, so the colours and textures should lend themselves to this. There is often a slight laziness within his character that changes after he climbs the beanstalk, so his clothes should reflect a more casual but heroic charm.

In *Dick Whittington* the audience knows from the outset that the hero will be made Lord Mayor of London but his clothes should not give the game away. So he should look poor and penniless at the beginning of the pantomime to contrast with his final ermine-clad Mayor. There is an inner confidence that should come through in his attire. So although penniless his rags should have some

style and not appear too jokey.

The hero as a girl

If sticking to tradition, the hero should be played by an actress dressed as a principal boy. As discussed previously in Chapter 2, this can be most effective when the heroes in question are more heroic than romantic. Jack and Dick fall into this category. Here there should be no facial changes, such as moustaches and beards and the hair, unless cut as a bob or elfin style, should be pulled back into a ponytail.

Baddies

The audience must know immediately that these are the evil characters. This is partly done though the costume design and use of certain significant

Working with the body shape

When designing the costume for a principal boy I never set out to disguise the fact that it is a woman playing the part! I design to the actress's assets. Design the tunic short enough to reveal a good amount of thigh but not so short that all of her modesty is revealed. Wearing a good pair of stunt pants or shorts over a pair of dance tights and dance fishnets helps the performer to feel secure and flatter the leg. Over-the-knee or thigh-length boots lengthen the leg but careful consideration needs to be paid as to the height and stability of the heel as the role of principal boy is physically demanding.

I always try to emphasize the shape of the female body with the principal boy's tunic or jacket through the tailoring. Squaring the shoulders with shoulder pads give a masculine line and height to the actress whilst still complementing her feminine body shape. Fabric choice is important. I choose fabrics with structure for the tunic but soft and flowing for the shirt.. think Mr Darcy!

Hair and make-up should not disguise the fact that this is a woman. Lighting can be very bright and colourful in pantomime, so emphasis on the eyes is very important, together with the cheekbones and lips.

Celia Perkins: set and costume designer

Amy Rhiannon Worth as Colin in Mother Goose *at Oldham Coliseum Theatre, showing the classic cut for the principal boy, pictured with Nicole Evans, Fine-Time Fontayne and Richard J. Fletcher; costume design by Celia Perkins; photography by Ian Tilton).*

colours – usually black, green and purple. Their hair tends to be dark, and on the men beards and moustaches can add to their evilness. Long cloaks with wicked collars (collars that are angular and designed to fan out around the neck) are an essential addition to the sinister persona. The cloak is also used extensively by the baddie to hide their face, loom up on people and to dramatically sweep on and off stage. Footwear for the baddie should extend the sinister look right down to the tip of their toes. Long, tight-fitting boots or shoes with spats can do this.

It is also useful to exaggerate their features through make-up, extending or changing the shape of eyebrows and even adding dark shading to the eyelids, which will draw attention to the eyes and make them look more evil.

The baddie's evil must contrast with the fairy's

Costume sketch for King Rat in Dick Whittington
and his Cat.

*Dale Superville as Wishee Washee in his loose-
fitting clothing and baseball boots, with Aladdin
played by Stefan Butler.*

goodness, so their costumes have to be at two extremes in terms of colours, fabrics and shapes. Whereas the fairy is quite soft and has curves, the baddie is harder and has a lot of angular shaping in the costume.

Comic character

It is important when clothing this character to remember that they will be one of the most active, so their clothing should be made from washable fabrics where possible, and be loose fitting so they will not feel restricted in their movement. Being a major protagonist in the slosh scene they are likely to get very messy, so they will require a duplicate costume to change into after these scenes.

The footwear is also important as they are constantly on the move. Putting them in trainers or baseball boots can really help them feel more secure. Having this type of footwear then dictates the style of costume which might go with them. It might seem odd to approach the character and design from the footwear up, but it is essential that they can be as active as the script and story demands. This is one character that can be dressed out of period and their clothing can provide a useful link with the audience.

Fabrics should be used in a comical manner with clashing colours and patterns to match their silly persona. It is important that these characters look comical and out of sync with the rest of the villagers/townspeople.

Magic/good characters

Because these characters epitomize goodness their costumes tend to use more pastel and light colours with lots of sparkle; they can be quirky but should still look beautiful and classical. There is purity in this character, which should be echoed in their clothes. The audience has to warm to the generosity of these characters almost instantaneously.

In quite a few of the pantomimes these characters are the Good Fairies and might hide their magical powers. This means that their costumes have to work on two levels: sparkly enough to look magical, but also normal enough to merge in with the rest of the townspeople.

Some of these Fairies will go through onstage transformation. Cinderella first meets her Fairy Godmother when she is disguised as an old woman in the forest and later reveals her true attire in the kitchen scene when she helps Cinderella prepare for the ball. This is often done with a specially designed cloak and ragged costume that can fall away to reveal her sparkly fairy outfit. The hood and part of the back of the cloak can be designed to split in half when pulled. Then, with the aid of a blackout and pyro-flash, the costume falls away from the head down and she can then step out of the heap that was the cloak/ragged attire.

In *Aladdin* there are two magical characters that help the hero. These are the Genie and the Spirit of the Ring, usually one male and one female. The Genie's magic is always more powerful than the Spirit of the Ring, and both characters tend to be more humorous than the traditional fairy. This allows the use of bolder colours and patterns which can be highly embellished with jewelling and sequins. Their outfits tend to be scanty with lots of flesh on show, which enables the use of

The Fairy Godmother in Cinderella, *disguised as the Old Woman and then revealed in all her sparkle (Gina Murray with Allyson Brown; photography by Manuel Harlan).*

Genie and Spirit of the Ring from **Aladdin** *(actors: Howard Coggins and Nicola Blackman; photography by Manuel Harlan).*

more expensive fabrics as you need only small amounts. This boldness of fabrics and colours also illustrates the fact that their magic is much more outwardly showy and sparks from them rather than from a magic wand or staff.

Heroine/love interest

The heroine is quite often as strong if not stronger than the hero in her braveness and confidence. Heroines are not just the pretty love interest for the hero but are more than able to look after themselves, and quite often make the hero struggle for their affection. For example, in *Aladdin* the Princess Baldroubadour can be quite feisty and be much more worldly than her more naive Aladdin, so by giving her Arabian-style bloomer trousers under a more feminine tunic can show both sides of the character. (It also makes it easier if she is wearing pants to sit appropriately on a flying carpet.)

Transformation from girl to woman

Most of the heroines bloom through the development of their story so the costumes should reflect this. With the character of Cinderella it is useful to look at how she grows in beauty and confidence through the way that the costumes are designed and cut. Because Cinderella is treated so

*Allyson Brown as Cinderella in her rags and then marrying her Prince Charming,
played by Oliver Tompsett.*

badly her first outfit should be rags. It is good to consider how these clothes might have looked before they became rags. Was Cinderella previously cared for and clothed well? Are the rags in fact a broken down version of what was once a beautiful dress?

When she is transformed into her ball gown by the Fairy Godmother there should still be a youthful quality: the ball gown should look radiant and sparkle under the lights as this is a magical outfit, but not show too much maturity. It is in her final wedding dress when she marries her Prince Charming that she can look more sophisticated and grown-up. One of the ways of doing this is to look at how the neckline and dress length can change with each new outfit. Both the neckline and hem length can become lower to highlight her growing maturity.

Adding another twist to the heroine

With their feisty nature comes the opportunity for them to create more humour and mayhem within the stories. The scenes with the hero and the baddie can become more fun when she is not the fawning romantic, or the willing victim. This makes her character much more active so the clothing also has to reflect this, and although fitted has to allow for more freedom. Length and fullness

91

The path of true love...

In our version of *Dick Whittington and his Cat*, Alice Fitzwarren disguises herself as Bob the Sailor to enable her to smuggle herself onto the ship with Dick. This is done through donning a principal boy style sailor's tunic and a small false moustache. This fools everybody, and causes an added complication when Dick finds himself strangely drawn to Bob, and both Bob (Alice) and Dick find it hard to hide their true emotions. This is made funnier because of the flimsy nature of the costumed disguise which in real life would fool nobody, and in fact the minute that she removes her moustache everyone (on stage) recognizes her.

Bob the Sailor, who is actually a disguised Alice Fitzwarren, pictured with Tommy the Cat in disguise as a parrot (Alice played by Sia Kiwa and Tommy played by Dale Superville).

of skirt need careful consideration to make sure no more than necessary is revealed.

Dame

The most unique character of all is that of the pantomime dame; in essence she captures the whole personality of pantomime. The artifice of having this motherly character played by a man immediately establishes that nothing can be taken too seriously. This cross-dressing has to be handled very carefully as it can be a fine line between the pantomime dame and drag/female impersonation. Whatever you do with the costumes and female shaping you must not completely conceal the man inside the frock.

It is also impossible to pigeon-hole or generalize about the dame as there are as many interpretations as there are performers who play the part. It is crucial that the performance style of the actor is studied carefully before deciding on how to clothe the character. The performer must feel comfortable with their female exterior and that their own personality, walk and movements are not completely lost or swamped by the costumes.

The dame is quite often very flirty with men within the audience. This is always playful and the absurd qualities within the costumes can help make this possible. Outrageously silly frocks help make the contact with men in the audience less threatening. Their playful sexual frustrations should always come from the characterization and script but never the costumes. The costumes are best when covering up the body but broadly exaggerating female assets, rather than revealing too much leg and flesh.

Boobs, bums and heels

Boob size can vary immensely. Some actors believe adding false boobs will take their characterization too far towards female impersonation. They very much want to appear as a man in a frock and want the shape to echo this. However, some say that they need something there to help them get into character. As most dames are motherly or matronly, boobs can help give them the right silhouette.

Sarah the Cook with her hands clenched under her boobs in a moment of disapproval (Howard Coggins in Dick Whittington and his Cat).

The dame is quite likely to show their underwear as part of the action. It is traditional that these are in the form of large cotton bloomers. Even when their outer attire is glamorous their smalls should remain the same overstated size. These should be in bright colours and patterns, and to add to the level of ridiculousness, they can even have slogans or comments printed or appliquéd on them.

In some cases the body padding can extend down from the boobs to include the bottom. Adding a full curvy bum can be useful if the character has close-fitting costumes. False bottoms can also be added directly into the backs of costumes. In this way the performer does not have to have the padding all the time which can help him cool down when changing between scenes. Where the costumes include full skirts then a large bum-roll added around the waist can give the skirt the desired kick-out.

Getting the footwear right is something that should be the choice of the performer in

Costume designs for Widow Twankey showing the exaggeration of shape through the width and fullness of sleeves and humorous emphasis on the 'larger size'.

Dale Superville during his first fitting, revelling in his padding and underwear for Ugly Sister 'Fruitella' in Cinderella; *Peter Shorey as Widow Twankey using Ping and Pong's police helmets to improve her womanly charms to beguile Abanazar in* Aladdin.

conversation with the designer and director. Some will want a small sturdy heel to give them a different sense of balance that they can then incorporate into the walk that they give their dame. Others will want to feel grounded – here even heavy-duty leather laced boots can be an option for footwear.

So many costumes
It is traditional that the dame has a costume change for every entrance that she makes. These usually begin with a more domestic-orientated outfit that describes their current financial status (usually poor), or their family business (as in *Aladdin* with Widow Twankey and her laundry). The dame is also one of the protagonists in the slosh scene so they will require one outfit (or part of an outfit) that is washable in case they get caught in the cross-fire. The other costumes are then designed to highlight subject matter within each scene they are entering; however, this link can be very tenuous, as it is more important that

Howard Coggins as Sarah the Cook dressed as a mermaid but still retaining her bloomers, tights and Doc Marten boots (pictured with Jeff Nicholson as Neptune; lighting design by John Harris).

the costume is comical than totally appropriate. What is really important is that each costume should top the previous in its scale and outrageousness with the walk-down costume being the most outlandish.

Because of the outrageous nature of the dame's costumes it can be fun to design outfits that are based on objects. Objects are funny because they are the last thing that you expect to see someone wearing as clothing. However, these can be difficult to move freely in, so should be chosen for the scenes where there is less movement. These can range from household objects right through to Christmas trees. In our version of *Cinderella* the Ugly Sister Adorabella's ball gown was designed as a tiered wedding cake with the statues of the bride and groom topping off the wig. This was very funny as an object but also fitted with her obsession to marry Prince Charming.

Maintaining a sense of the character

It is very easy to get carried away with the

95

Adorabella's 'wedding cake' costume in **Cinderella** *(played by Kieran Buckeridge).*

their more mature counterparts in the other pantomimes.

• Quite often the dame is the mother to the central character, so although at times outrageous, her costumes should reflect her maternal persona. The characters of Widow Twankey (mother to Aladdin), Dame Trott (mother to Jack), and Mother Goose all profess severe poverty at the beginning of their stories, so their costumes should reflect this – not necessarily rags, but costumes that incorporate panto patches (squares of fabric with obvious large black stitch lines). They are often the sole parent so are working mums, meaning that their costumes have to reflect their working profession as well as their personality.

• With *Dick Whittington*, *Babes in the Wood* and *Sleeping Beauty* the dame is more a nursemaid or nanny-type character, which again requires the inclusion of their professional role as well as a more matronly quality. These characters are often spinsters or divorcees, enabling them to openly flirt with men in the audience.

Hairdos and slap

The hair for the dame should look as false as possible (an obvious wig). Very neatly coiffured hair can work against the dame's personality. A more ramshackle and quickly achieved style will fit the character better. Keeping to the same hair colouring throughout is useful: the dame goes through so many costume changes that it can get confusing for the young children in the audience if there is not some continuity in their appearance.

The wigs can be highly coloured and oversized or, as in their traditional past, a more sombre grey-haired wig pulled back into a bun. The type of wig will depend on the particular image that the actor is putting across – be it 'mutton dressed as lamb' or more of a bloke in a frock – either can work well.

Wigs don't always need to be complete hairpieces as the dame can wear a plethora of mop caps and headgear. Hairpieces attached to these can be all that is required. It is also more comfortable for the actor to not have to wear a full wig all the time.

absurdity, scale and possibilities that are open when designing the dame's frocks. However, you must make careful note of several things:

• Firstly, the dame is not simply a 'clothes horse' to parade a series of outrageous outfits. The dame is an important character within the story. The audience must believe in the truth and generally warm-hearted nature of the character. Even in *Cinderella* the Ugly Sisters are often more misguided than evil, and their outfits can appear more outwardly flirty than

Due to the excessive taking off and putting on of wigs, and the number of performances, dames' wigs are often permanently set using varnish. This adds to the false quality and means that the wig will need very little attention throughout the entire run of the pantomime. With this permanently set style of wig it is also easy to clip in additions to change the look for different scenes. With very large wigs and headdresses a felt head-block fitted inside the wig and an elasticated chin-strap might be required to make them more secure.

How much the face is made up is dependent upon the dame's individual characterization. Some dames like to use very little make-up and will use their own facial contortions to express the character. It is widely recorded that when comedian Les Dawson did pantomime, dabs of rouge on the end of the nose and the cheeks were all he did to capture his dame.

Some dames' make-up can be at the other extreme where it is almost full Restoration/clown make-up. Whichever type is chosen, it must look imperfect and bizarre. Perfectly drawn lips and matching eye shades and blushers can make it look too close to drag. Go for clashing colours and bolder, freely drawn shapes. Highlight imperfections such as moles and bulbous noses. Pursed, tiny lips and raising the eyebrows can be a really effective means of exaggeration. It is worth the actor experimenting with their own make-up during the rehearsal period, trying out different possibilities to get it right for them, the designer and the audience.

Animal friends/skin parts

There are several animal friends that are integral characters within certain stories. The way in which costumes are designed for these will reflect as much the character that inhabits them as the animal that they are portraying. Is the animal cute, cuddly and comical, or sleek and sophisticated? An example of the most apparent difference is with Dick Whittington's cat: he or she can be played by a dancer and be sleek and silent or a comic actor and be brash and bold. The fabrics and construction of these outfits will be

The varnished wig for Fruitella in Cinderella, *with a doughnut headdress simply pinned in.*

97

Costume designs for Tommy the Cat in **Dick Whittington.**

substantially different depending on which version you choose.

An immensely important consideration with all of them is comfort. Some will only be on stage in one or two scenes, but some have to inhabit these costumes for the entire pantomime. If possible make sure the costumes are made from fabrics that can breathe. The weight of the costume should be kept to a minimum, so avoid heavy fur fabric that will insulate and become hot for the performer after a very short space of time. Another great alternative can be strips of clipped fabric that can be sewn on in layers to create a fur or feather effect. This type of costume can also be made washable so if it gets sweaty it can be rinsed through.

Design for all of these costumes must have detachable heads so that as soon as the performer

leaves the stage they can remove them to cool down. In big costumes small battery-operated fans can be fitted to help with cooling. Having separate heads for these characters can allow hat or headdress changes by having duplicate heads.

Considering the shape of the animal
Where possible try to echo the shape of the particular animal in the structuring of the costume. With a cat, lengthening the body and losing the hips will help create the right shape. With cows and horses and camels, which are invariably done using two performers (front and back ends), one person stands upright while the other is bent over and holds onto the waist of the person in front. This creates a downward slope of the back that can look odd.

When creating the body for a cow think about making a cage-like shape for this rather than simply having a fabric drape; it will give a more realistic contour and help by making it less claustrophobic for the actor who is the back. With cows you can even attach a working udder to the underside of this cage so that the cow can squirt milk on cue. This cage is best made from foam as the animal will need to bend and even possibly sit down.

Hooped structures

Shapes can also be made through a series of hoops, which are linked to create the required framework and then covered in a skin of fabric to which the outer layer can be attached. This is really useful if the animal friend has to move freely and the body flex with them. This was used when creating the hen that lays the golden eggs for *Jack and the Beanstalk*. The actress playing the hen was trained in ballet and could do parts of the action on point so this type of structure was light enough for her to dance in, but strong enough to keep its shape. The ragged fabric-feathered skin, although time consuming, gave lots of movement and ruffled as the dancer's moves got more frantic.

Visibility

It is important that the performers inside the animal costumes can see clearly. With animal characters that have structured/enclosed heads it is important to design cut-away panels for them to see through. These can be gauzed and painted to blend in with the rest of the costume. But it is important that they are able to see to the front and if possible both sides. This will help them get on and off without the risk of colliding with the set or other characters.

With animals that have faces in the same place as the actor then it is best to use the performer's face and apply make up to create noses, whiskers, etc. It is much better for the audience to see the expressions created by the performer. A false head/face can at times appear quite lifeless.

Status characters

As mentioned previously it is important that these characters' 'badges of office' are clearly visible for all the audience to understand. So kings and queens should be decked in lavish fabrics trimmed in ermine, and should sport crowns. Pantomime stories usually treat royalty and persons of high status with a certain amount of disdain, so the use of fabrics although sumptuous should be treated in

Daisy the Cow in Jack and the Beanstalk *doing one of her tricks (played by Alice Jackson and Martine Burt).*

The hen from Jack and the Beanstalk *showing the feathered structure (Alice Jackson being fitted by the maker Tina Kennedy) and in production, the hen going onto 'points' (lighting design by John Harris).*

a more comical than regal manner and they should appear overdressed for every occasion. This might extend into their hair and make-up, with highly styled and set wigs with ruddy cheeks and red noses.

Comedy sidekicks

These characters usually have some form of authority that is handed down to them by status characters or the baddie, but they are totally inept and will mess up every task with hilarious results.

In pairings such as the Broker's Men or the more obvious pairings of Ping and Pong, the Chinese policemen in *Aladdin*, it can be fun to play with matching costumes, particularly when their shapes and sizes differ massively. A great deal of humour can be gained from one of the pairing's outfit not fitting them, or being more ridiculous than the other. This echoes the idea of the straight man and the fool in classic comedy duos.

When it is a single character they are usually attached to the baddie as a foil to their evilness and scariness. They can defuse moments when the baddie might be having a manic rant that might otherwise scare the youngsters, by using physical humour or saying something totally inappropriate and silly. Their costumes are likely to be very similar in treatment to the comic character discussed earlier.

Characters that are objects

It can be fun to play with the idea of giving supposedly inanimate objects characters. These can be made as hand props/puppets and manipulated by characters within the stories, but a lot of fun can be gained by making them a prop costume inhabited by a performer.

Two such objects are the hen that lays the golden eggs (discussed earlier), and the Giant's magical harp in *Jack and the Beanstalk*. It is this magical harp that comforts the Giant, singing him or her off to sleep, enabling Jack to escape. To animate a hand-prop, LEDs can be set into the body of the harp to flash in time with the music, whereas a prop costume version can allow the performer to sing and strum their own strings. This gives the harp much more scope for characterization. In our version (pictured) the costume was designed to parody the animated household objects in Walt Disney's *Beauty and the Beast*.

King Rat's sidekick, Nat-the-Rat in Dick Whittington and his Cat *(played by Natasha Cox).*

The harp played by Martine Burt in Jack and the Beanstalk *(costume made by John Brooking; lighting design by John Harris).*

7 CREATING THE COSTUMES

Having begun to look at how the writing and design work together to create the 'open stage' and the beginnings of the characters and costumes it is now time to move on to look at how all the design and production elements work together to hone the storytelling and create the show.

No matter what scale or budget, the realization of the costumes is of paramount importance. The set can be pared down to the bare minimum, but the characters required to tell the story cannot. Costume can carry the entire design aesthetic. You could do a pantomime in a hospital ward or a shopping centre as long as the costumed characters embody the traditions and storytelling required of pantomime.

Having stated how important the costumes are, they can also be the aspect of the production that often gets left till after the set is finished. This can in part be attributed to waiting on the casting, or, more dangerously, because they are seen as a random collection of comical clothing that can be put together with little consideration of their relationship to each other, the set, or historic period. Nothing could be further from the truth.

There are numerous decisions that can and should be made alongside the development of the

script and set design. Designing the costumes once the set is at the 'open stage' point means that the

Costume for Dame Felicity Trott in Jack and the Beanstalk, *showing how the idea of leisurewear can be taken to the extreme and create its own visual humour (Dame played by Christopher Robert pictured with members of the junior chorus).*

OPPOSITE: *Andrew Bolton being fitted by costume maker Elizabeth Waters for his King's costume in* Cinderella.

theatre space has been established enough to make some costume decisions, and also promotes the process of designing set and costumes alongside each other so that they can grow together as well as informing the writing.

An enjoyable aspect of designing pantomime costumes is that they can be a joke in their own right, even delivering their own visual punchline. They can also parody local people from the town or community, famous people, or celebrities who have been in the news in the last twelve months.

Some costumes can be completely out of period and still work. This is because audiences are always aware that what they are watching is a theatrical event. A pantomime is an interpretation of an old fairy story, and because of this it is perfectly acceptable to have modern fashion trends (with pantomime touches) without seeming out of place, because the pantomime performance exists in both the present and the fairytale past.

What defines a pantomime costume?

Heightened sense of reality

Costuming pantomime is very different from clothing any other productions; it is important that they don't ever become too naturalistic. The use of colours, fabrics and styles should be brave, brash

Jill McSpotty, played by Natasha Cox in Jack and the Beanstalk, *showing how the cut, fabric and colour take this costume away from reality by echoing, rather than copying a period (costume sketch drawn by Emma Morton).*

and 'in your face'. High street fashion can be parodied, but should not be used straight off the shelf.

The structure of the dialogue/jokes and narrative pushes for humour and wit throughout all the costume designs, to a varying degree. Inevitably certain characters such as the dame will have their completely outrageous outfits that stand out from the rest of the company, but even they must have some visual association to the other characters' clothes. After all, she is quite often someone's mother or nursemaid.

Fixing a time period

There can be huge amounts of 'artistic licence' in how the designs adhere to a period of history, but it must feel rooted somewhere, or the audience will be in danger of losing the sense of place. It is important to consider the type of the story – is it heroic or romantic? Recognizing which can help you decide. Another reason for choosing a particular period concerns the expectation that the audiences have about certain characters and their clothes. Cinderella's ball gown is a prime example. All the little girls in the audience will feel let down if Cinderella's gown is not a classic ball gown shape (frothy, sparkly and based on a crinoline), no matter how well it is designed to fit with a more modern time period. Remember you are working as much with expectation as personal creative choices, and at times you have to trust the established protocols and not push for re-invention.

Magical transformations

Some costumes will need to transform before the audience's eyes. Characters such as Cinderella, the Fairy Godmother, Aladdin and Mother Goose all go through transformations from rags to riches or old age to youthful beauty. The audience, and especially the younger ones, should be amazed at how these transformations have occurred.

It can be done by designing a costume that will fall away to reveal the beautiful outfit underneath, but is more commonly done by having a double. At some point in the action the character has to exit offstage, putting a cloak on to cover their head, and more importantly their face. Once they are offstage, they switch, and the double then does the next entrance (usually upstage so that attention is not drawn to them). The real character can add the voice where necessary from offstage, whilst they are being changed into their transformed outfit. Then with the help of a black-out and pyro flash the two can switch back and it appears that they have instantaneously transformed. The switch can be aided in the design of the set by the use of secret panels/trap doors, and so on.

These transformations are always tricky to get right but should not be overlooked or edited out of the pantomime as they are one of things that the audiences expect to see.

DESIGN

Choosing the colour palette

Because pantomime has such a unity within its design, it is really important to look at how the set and costumes work with each other in terms of colour. Usually the set leads some of the decision-making concerning colour, but there should always be a consideration of what colours might be essential for the costumes. Certain pantomime characters have pre-ordained colours, either due to direct association with the particular character (such as Robin Hood in Lincoln Green) or are colours that subliminally or traditionally suggest certain character types such as black, green and purple for the baddie. Although you can decide to work against tradition it is important to know you are doing this, and consider how it might come across to your audience.

Use of complementary colours can provide complete contrast between the set and costumes. For example in our production of *Aladdin*, the portals and most of the floor were a deep cobalt blue, so oranges, reds and yellows were used in the opening chorus costumes so that it created the biggest contrast.

Fabric sampling

It is good to do fabric sampling as part of the design

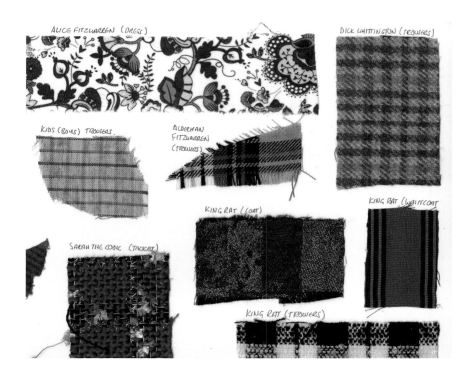

ALICE FITZWARREN (DRESS)

DICK WHITTINGTON (TROUSERS)

KIDS (BOYS) TROUSERS

ALDERMAN FITZWARREN (TROUSERS)

KING RAT (WAISTCOAT)

KING RAT (COAT)

SARAH THE COOK (JACKET)

KING RAT (TROUSERS)

Fabric samples collected by the designer for Dick Whittington and his Cat, *prior to beginning the designs.*

Dame Felicity Trott's alarm clock outfit for Jack and the Beanstalk *made from Plastazote foam and PVC (actor: Christopher Robert).*

process. This is to make sure that as a designer you are aware of the cost of fabrics and the availability. Fabrics, like fashion, can change with the seasons and the years, so what might have been available last year may have gone out of style. Bear in mind that this sampling will be 'out of season' and that some of the winter fabrics (sequins, glitter and fur) may not be as abundant until closer to Christmas. With such fabrics as velvets and cotton drill it might be more economical to order by the roll, especially if you are using these for chorus or an entire set of walk-down costumes.

It is incredibly important to look at the size of pattern on fabrics; small patterns and some textures will not work well for pantomime. Subtle patterns and colours will get lost against the painted set. Use bold patterns and coloured fabrics and mix them up as much as possible. The quirky nature of pantomime requires equal quirkiness in the way you mix and match fabrics and colours.

It is important to choose fabrics that are washable and colour-fast so you don't get one colour running into another during the frequent

Large costume props

The main demand from any performer is a lightweight costume in which they can easily move. However, this becomes a challenge when asked to make a costume representing a large pork pie, cake, washing machine, or full English breakfast.

I have used everything from cane to steel to create large shapes. Sometimes less traditional materials are the right solution for the job. Large carved blocks of foam rubber can be just right if you are making a giant doughnut.

A lot of character and prop costumes are made of Plastazote: a lightweight, flexible but also rigid foam. Plastazote comes in a variety of colours and thicknesses starting at 3mm and progressing in increments of 3mm to 18mm. It can be laminated and with the application of heat will stick to itself. A glue gun can be used for this purpose. It can be vacuum-formed and curved with the careful use of a heat gun over a positive mould. The foam shape is then covered in fabric, or can be painted any colour with an initial application of a flexible textured paint.

John Brooking: designer

Fried breakfast frock for Arthur Bostrum as Sarah the Cook in Dick Whittington *at Stafford Gatehouse Theatre (costume design by John Brooking; photography by Robert Day).*

washes. These striking fabrics are quite often not the most expensive. Even on the largest of budgets, you can't always afford high-quality fabrics due to the sheer volume of costume makes. With such fabrics as imitation silk, it will actually look better and last longer than silk itself. It is worth buying the best quality of satin, however, as it tends to be thicker and will be more durable and keep its sheen throughout the run.

If non-washable fabrics are used then it is important to design appropriate washable undergarments. A lot of the man-made fabrics will make the performer perspire and cotton undergarments will help avoid staining the outer costumes.

For pantomime you will need to look to a wide range of fabrics, some of which might be quite alien to costume making – things such as plastic tablecloths and artificial grass, rubber and foam. All of these can be employed to add structure and texture to the more outrageous frocks, such as those worn by the dame.

Layering of fabrics can be really successful to get a depth of colour and surface sparkle. Use organzas and sequin net over shot or single-colour satins to create magical effects for ball gowns and fairy tutus, which might otherwise require very expensive fabrics and never add as much depth of colour and texture.

Lighting considerations

The choice of fabrics should always bear in mind the quality of the stage lighting. It is not usually possible to discuss the fabrics with the lighting designer at the sampling stage, so it is worth the costume designer experimenting with their sample fabrics. Illuminate them with gels from a lighting gel swatch book, using a torch as a light source, to see how fabrics react under different colours. Certain colours go very murky and unattractive in coloured light.

It is particularly important to consider the time of day within the scenes, as this will influence the choice of colours. If the scene takes place at night then it will inevitably be using cooler washes with strong blues, so colours will need to work with these hues. Some of the main characters can be lit with a follow spot, so their costumes can be freer in their choice of colours than the rest of the ensemble.

INITIAL DESIGN SKETCHES

Quick sketching a 'costume parade'

Before going into detail with individual characters it is good to get them all sketched out, in appropriate groupings, on a single sheet of paper. These are not intentionally done as preliminary costume designs but are much more about the shape and heights of the characters with a hint of

The working drawing (costume parade) for some of the characters in Dick Whittington and his Cat. *These were developed by sketching and erasing till both designer and writer/director were happy to continue on to the finished designs.*

Student designer/costume maker Lisa Else beginning to transfer her quick drawings onto her pre-prepared character worksheets.

possible costume. This is a really useful tool to open up discussions with the writer/director about shared perceptions of the look of the characters. Seeing these figures more as shapes can begin to question how they relate to each other and because they are drawn so quickly, are based on instinctive responses rather than carefully considered designs. Sometimes these instinctive drawings progress right through to finished designs.

These can be chatted over, erased or amended as the discussions are occurring. Then, gradually, small rough pencil sketches for the costumes begin to appear. It is also a means of gaining confidence when dealing with what might be up to a hundred costumes. Knowing that you have just an initial rough sketch for all the characters makes the task of completing the costumes seem less daunting.

Initial individual sketches

To begin sketching out more detailed costume designs there must be a good shared understanding between the writer/director and the designer as to who these characters are. This might go as far as looking at possible casting (ideas about casting tend to be led by a casting director or by the director). However, ideas can develop as a direct result of the character shapes explored in the 'costume parade sketch'. Once characters are cast, their faces and stature can be incorporated into the design sketches.

It can be good to find ways of incorporating the costume and character research onto the costume sketches. One good way is to take each character and scan in the research and reference pictures and then create worksheets, with the images taking up part of the page and leaving a large gap to start the drawing. This will mean your references are always to hand and you eliminate the problem of facing the blank page. These sketch sheets will show the makers not only the final sketch, but where those ideas were developed from, which can be very useful when interpreting the designs.

Mixing the modern and period

I did costumes for Kim and Aggie, the TV cleaning ladies, for which I created period 'panniers' (side 'baskets' on seventeenth-century dresses) made completely out of household rubber gloves, thus taking something modern and making it period.

These celebrities said it is always important to be seen wearing their trademark rubber gloves. It was my responsibility as designer to take that to a higher level and give them something that was less obvious and altogether more quirky.

Terry Parsons: set and costume designer

'Trademark' costumes

There are professional dames who sometimes come with their own set of costumes, so these have to be discussed with the performer to discover relevant moments for inclusion within the story. This is always possible because the dame's outfits are usually based on themes, objects and jokes and designed for generic scenes that many pantomimes have, such as the cooking or laundry scene.

In some cases actors might have been contracted before the design begins and have an already established interpretation for a particular pantomime character. For example an actor/comedian might have a trademark item of clothing that will need incorporating into their costume designs.

Checking for movement

It is useful to jot down the sort of movement each character might make. This will have an input into the shape and length of costumes. If the character is very energetic then he or she might need loose-fitting garments and shoes that provide decent grip. Does the baddie slink or sweep onto stage? If he does, he will almost certainly require a long cloak. The lengths can also be dictated by what actions they have: hectic dances will require full-length frocks to finish just above the floor to avoid tripping over the hem. But it should always be remembered that dance will play an important part so every costume will have to allow for this.

Traditional costume shapes and detailing

There are certain details on costumes that are signifiers, such as Kings and Queens having crowns; royalty and Lord Mayors having ermine trim; dames having aprons to hold sweets, handkerchiefs, and so on. Poor characters inevitably have pantomime stitched patches on their otherwise normal clothes. These are key signifiers in pantomime costume which can be easily read by young and old in the audience.

The shape of the clothing should be as exaggerated as the colours and fabrics. If a skirt is full it should be obviously so, quite often using full circle. Sleeves if puffed should be larger than life, and if costumes are designed to look ill-fitting then they should be visibly so; however, making them tight might prove too restricting. It is a matter of remembering the storybook style of the clothes and making sure this carries right through to the finished garments.

It is also worth checking what might be available for hire that matches with the design concept, or even sends the design in a different direction. Found or hired costumes can sometimes save vast amounts of making time and help bring the costumes in on budget. Some theatres and costume hire companies have a stock of pantomime costumes; they might also have some period clothes made in non-traditional fabrics which could also be suitable.

Shell suit costume taken straight off the rail at Birmingham Costume Hire with wardrobe supervisor Kirsty Rowe.

In our production of *Dick Whittington* there was a discussion between director, designer and production manager (Ali Fellows) about what costumes might be right for the dame in the underwater scene. We knew we wanted it to be 'urban teenage' with some references to the sea, but we weren't sure what. 'A "shell" suit?!' quipped Ali. We loved it, and decided we would indeed go with a kind of 1980s tracksuit covered in shells. When sourcing other costumes at Birmingham Costume Hire, a perfect match for our concept was discovered hanging on the hire rails – proving that nothing is ever truly original, but that you should always keep your eyes and your options open. You never know what 'gem' might be out there!

MOVING ON TO THE FINAL COSTUME DESIGNS

Having got the initial pencil sketches of the characters it is now time to move on to the final costume designs. You should check with the costume makers in case there is a particular order they want to receive them in. It is often useful to leave the dame till last, as with this character you really do need to know who has been cast, before making final costume decisions. The way an actor will approach the dame will be very personal and the costumes have to take this into consideration.

Costume designs for the Ugly Sisters in Cinderella *in gouache and coloured marker pen (designed by Terry Parsons for First Family Entertainment).*

Choosing the right style and medium for the final costume sketches

Final sketches can be left as simple as a line drawing of the costume with fabric swatches pinned to them to give ideas of colour and pattern. However, full-colour costumes (if time allows) can provide more information.

Creating full-colour versions communicate to the writer/director and lighting designer the final colours with more clarity. If a costume is being made by a freelancer there might be little or no opportunity to visit them in person, so telephone discussions using the full colour design will be hugely beneficial. Then, when it comes to buying fabrics, the coloured costume sketches can be used by the wardrobe supervisor to draw up a shopping list of fabrics, and act as an aide-memoire during the actual shopping trips. Even when it might be the designer who is doing that shopping, it could be several months since the costumes were originally drawn and the colours and ideas for fabrics can be forgotten in the mists of time.

The style of line and colour can be more cartoon-like, as this reflects the style of the genre, but even if using a more realistic rendering for your figures, the colours should be strong and bold. When adding the colour to the sketches, experiment with the clashing of colours and patterns as discussed previously.

If the colours are to be rendered by hand, use coloured markers or gouaches to get the intensity of colour. These final sketches can also be done using a computer drawing program such as Photoshop: here you can scan in the line drawing of the costume and add the colours or photographic images of fabrics as layers to experiment and come up with the final costume sketches. The joy of this process is that you can repeatedly change colours as many times as you want without having to redraw the character's body and shape of the costume. It can initially take longer than drawing by hand, but if you are less certain of your colours and patterns then this method can be most useful.

DESIGNING HAIR AND MAKE-UP

The hair and make-up are the finishing touches that complete the character's look. It is useful to consider where possible using the actor's own hair as wigs can not only be expensive, but they also require maintenance and can be very hot if worn throughout the production. However, they can be very useful if your actor is playing more than one character, as a wig can make an instant change to someone's look (be it length or colour) and help the audience understand the different characters more clearly.

Wigs can also help establish historic periods: for example if setting *Cinderella* in the seventeenth or eighteenth century, then the formal wigs and make-up of those periods can be utilized for the ball scene to get the required formality; and for a medieval version of *Dick Whittington* the plaited and ornate hair-buns of that period can be both comical and authentic.

As previously mentioned, the baddie can have additional facial hair such as a beard and long moustache that he can swirl in his fingers. The Giant in *Jack and the Beanstalk* usually has a full beard. In some productions this will be on a puppet head, where the beard will help disguise the movement of the mouth. Where the Giant is an actor, it is likely that he will be playing another character in the first act, so a beard and wig can change the shape and size of his face to make him look completely different.

With other characters, changing the colour and style of their hair can make them appear much more pantomime-like. For Mayor Dotty McSpotty in *Jack and the Beanstalk*, a blue-rinse wig was created to give her a more severe and Thatcheresque quality.

ALTERATIONS

With pantomime the costume designs and the making come much earlier than the rehearsal period, so the decisions concerning costumes are fixed at the design stage with less possibility for

Styling real hair wigs for pantomime

Wig-making has changed very little in hundreds of years. We make use of modern foundation materials but there is no definitive substitute for natural hair. Certainly synthetic wigs are used for pantomime, but these are not so malleable and cannot be fashioned into such wonderful creations as purpose-made wigs of natural hair. Natural hair can be bleached and dyed to any colour, and it can be permed, curled and set into any shape required. The shape and size of the wig should be in balance with the costume and the hair colour should reflect the character. Evil or 'baddie' roles might be black or darkest brown; the heroine, blonde; a good fairy, silver or white; and a wizard, red and so on. There is also plenty of scope for ancillary roles to be portrayed with blue or green hair, perhaps to complement a costume.

With the cross-dressed characters I carefully knot a female hairline (rounded in shape) for the dame or any man playing a female role, and a male hairline (with recedes) for, say, the principal boy.

In *Cinderella*, if traditionally set in eighteenth-century costume, the wigs for the walk-down scene are made with white yak animal hair. Built on a normal foundation, but to achieve the height required for eighteenth-century wigs, one would make a cage from malleable wire that is covered in a lightweight fabric; onto the fabric, wefts of hair or hair pieces are stitched. The cage is added to the wig and the hair on the wig and the hair on the cage are blended together, curled and pinned into the required (oversized) shape.

Felicite Gillham: freelance wig designer

The real hair beard for the Giant in Jack and the Beanstalk, *which was blended to match his own long hair (actor: Richard Ashton; beard designed and created by Felicite Gillham).*

change or sourcing alongside the rehearsal process.

In some cases the cost or availability of certain fabrics might prohibit sticking to the original plans. Also, when completing the casting of the roles it might mean that certain colours, patterns or even shapes of costumes have to change to accommodate the performer's shape and size. Even when the performers are in rehearsals, ideas for movements and dancing can mean that certain aspects of the costume have to be adapted. It is impossible to predict all this when the costumes are originally conceived, so creative flexibility and speedy decision-making is required right up until the pantomime opens.

Quick costume changes

There will be a high predominance of costumes that will need to be designed and made for quick changes. This is particularly important for the

Costume for Dame Trott, showing the layers sewn together already in the first fitting (Christopher Robert with maker Dawn Evans), and the final costume onstage.

Making allowance for speedy and quiet changes

Because pantomime costumes can be complex, with things such as crinolines, padding and multiple layers to outfits, you have to first think how the person can get out of it quickly and quietly. This means not using masses of noisy Velcro because the audience will hear it. If using zip fasteners, make sure that they are the chunky variety, as they are less likely to catch or jam when hurried.

Sew as much of the costume together as possible, because if you have got a costume with too many layers this will cause problems for quick changes: the more layers you have, the more dressers you need,

and one each side of stage is usually all that can be afforded.

Dames will quite often have complete padded bodies to create the right shape, which they wear all the way through the show under their other costumes. This will help with the quick changes but has an impact on maintenance. They can get very sweaty, and if the performer has only one padded body he will end up putting on a cold and damp suit, which is not nice at all. So it is worth considering a second body, so that they can be rotated: one onstage whilst the other is in the wash and drying.

Kirsty Rowe: wardrobe supervisor

dame, who has more complex costumes and quick changes for her many entrances. It is important to predict quick changes at the design stage wherever possible.

GETTING COSTUMES READY FOR THE FIRST PERFORMANCE

It is quite simply an enormous task to get such a vast number of costumes ready in time for first night/matinée. In the writing of the pantomime and the designing of the costumes it is crucial that you consider the resources that will be available to make all these costumes. In regional theatre some costumes will be made in-house and some may be sent out to freelance costume makers, so the sketches and costings have to be as thorough and complete as possible to avoid confusion or overspend.

Due to the time frame, there are few fittings for pantomime actors, and many costumes are almost complete when they are tried on for the first time. As Kirsty Rowe, wardrobe supervisor explains:

You work from their measurements and tend to leap straight into cutting the fabric and make it up to a first or even second fitting stage, making sure that you leave enough seam allowance and adjustments all over. It can look quite silly when doing the fitting as the actor thinks it is huge, but it is so much easier to make the costume that little bit bigger just in case and then take it in during the fitting.

This process is anticipated by most actors who work in pantomime – they know they are going to have less say in how their costumes look. This is something that the designer has to be sensitive to in the fittings, to make sure that the actors feel listened to, but that no major changes occur that might jeopardize getting the costumes finished.

The dame is the one character where the performer should be involved more closely in development. Those playing the dame (who don't have already existing frocks) will need to have all their costumes designed and made especially for them. So, from my experience, they like to be consulted on how these are going to fit with their personality and stature. This can be done by scanning and emailing images of the early pencil sketches so that they can then be discussed and adapted via email or phone, at a time in the process when it is easier to make changes. They will also require a full half-day set aside in the rehearsal process to do just their costume fittings.

Getting everything finished

The costumes are quite often made in the order that they appear onstage. It is quite usual to have begun the technical rehearsals when the walk-down outfits are still being made and decorated. Somehow this process, although stressful, seems part of theatre tradition. There is something truly magical in seeing characters appear at the top of the finale staircase in costumes that were on the stand only hours previously.

Finally, it is worth noting that the costumes rely heavily on highly skilled makers. You can have the best costume designs ever, but if the interpretation of these is not as creative, and the patterns, cutting and tailoring are less than perfect, then the costumes and the demeanour of the actors will suffer. The quality of the costumes is very important to the actors. They feel creatively

---

Discovering the costume's importance

It is often only when an actor steps in front of an audience that they discover the real value of a well-thought-through character costume. As an example Christopher Robert (Dame Felicity Trott in *Jack and the Beanstalk*) states: 'I only realized the true importance of my costumes once I was in front of an audience: just entering in the outfits got an instant response. My costumes did so much to immediately establish my character.' Comments like this let the team know when the design, the making and the script have blended seamlessly to create the perfect costumed pantomime character.

supported in well-designed and conceived costumes. They could be doing over fifty shows within a short time frame with multiple changes, so it is crucial that their costumes are impressive, comfortable and made to withstand the rigours of the production, looking as good on the last night as they did on the first.

One of the costume designs for Dame Felicity Trott, which was thoroughly discussed with the actor from rough pencils right through to the finished costume.

Dame Trott
JACK AND THE BEANSTALK

ACT 1 Milk scene

8 SET, PROP AND FURNITURE DESIGN

With pantomime existing in two time frames – the present day of the performance and the artificial world of the fairytale – the stage design is mainly rooted in the latter of these, but makes references to the present.

The designer should inject their own personal wit in the way that the settings retell the traditional stories and, together with the writer/director, come to conclusions about how scenes will work spatially. The designer should also consider how the visual transformations might occur within and between scenes alongside the writing process. Examples of this collaboration will be evident throughout this chapter.

THE DESIGN PREPARATION

A good level of drawing and painting skills is crucial in designing a pantomime. Very few other types of production require the same amount of drawn artwork. It is the one genre where absolutely everything that appears on stage has to be designed, from the scenery right down to the smallest of hand props. It is very rare that anything sourced or bought from a shop will be able to go onstage without it being 'pantomized'. The artificiality and oversized nature of pantomime

OPPOSITE: *Scenic artist Christabel Cant painting the scenery for Widow Twankey's Laundry in Aladdin.*

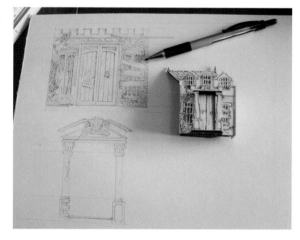

Photograph showing the 1:50 scale sketch model of Hardup Hall for Cinderella together with 1:25 scale pencil drawings of the fascias in preparation for the final model.

design needs to be evident throughout.

It is also really important to utilize one's own drawing and painting style and not try to echo any other designer's work. There is so much to design that in order to cope with the sheer volume the drawing needs to come naturally.

The model for Aladdin. *Notice how on this example the line work uses darker shades of the block colours rather than black, giving a softer effect.*

The use of the Arabian dome shape for the portals and the set for Aladdin *helps to establish the location.*

Deciding on the historic period and architecture

It is true that any choice of historic period is a possibility, and that the interpretation of this period can be loose, but the pantomime world should always be rooted in a historic period as a starting point. This is something that the creative team must decide right at the beginning of the process, even before the design of the 'open stage'. It is important because the tone and references in the script and set may well draw facts and humour from a specific period of history as well as current places and trends. It becomes interesting when parallels can be drawn between now and then.

It is unlikely that pantomime design will follow the rules of architecture precisely, but quite often archways, columns, doors and windows are used to indicate a particular architectural period, and through the way they are drawn, are subverted into pantomime versions of classical details. Certain architectural details can be very iconic and help establish location, sometimes by shape alone. With *Aladdin*, for example, taking the onion-shaped domes and minarets of Arabian countries can instantly establish where we are.

Line and colour

Scenic cloths and set are usually 'lined in' (the design has black, grey or coloured lines that define the details on the design). This is very traditional and helps create the storybook quality. The quality of this line work (solid or broken, sketchy or precise, bold or fine) is where the designer can add their own style.

Use of colour is also important. Are strong colours or pastel shades to be used? How is the paint applied – is it as solid blocks of colour, blended, or as washes? These things need to be very clear in your design and finished model so that the interpretation in the final painting can match the desired effect.

It is worthwhile playing with and developing your own style of drawing and painting by taking a photographic reference of a location and continually redrawing it until you are happy that you have established a style that suits the particular pantomime, and that can be sustained throughout the whole design.

Children's storybooks are an ideal source of reference, as they are something that younger audiences are already familiar with; children find it fascinating seeing a storybook-style set come to life.

Not all pantomime designs are designed with the youngsters in mind: some have more adult reference points. In approaching *Dick Whittington*

Reference image and line drawing of the theatre frontcloth for **Dick Whittington and his Cat.**

121

Using vastly contrasting colours against a set with a limited palette can make characters 'zing' out (actors: Dale Superville and Christopher Robert; lighting design by John Harris).

Use of colour in set and costume

When designing the set and costumes for pantomime I tend to use a bolder, more intense colour palette for the costumes and tonally lighten that palette in the set. Visually I feel this ensures that the performers don't merge into the scenery in what can be a very busy stage. With so much going on – loud music, eye-popping scenery, bright or moving lights – the palettes I use help the performers and their costumes stand out.

In the past I have used coloured lining – in on the set rather than black lines, utilizing black with bold colours on the costumes. I have also used contrasting colours for the sets and costumes – all as a device to lift the costumes visually from the set.

Celia Perkins: set and costume designer

---

and his Cat at Watford Palace Theatre we were tasked with celebrating the theatre's centenary. Here we went back to Victorian etchings as a primary source of research. A design was

developed in which all the scenery had an etched quality.

Whichever age group the design is aimed at, remember that it is a family show that must capture the imagination of young and old through the drawings and colours that you choose.

Deciding on a colour palette

Full colour can be used on the set, but it is best to consider holding back some colours from that palette to use solely on the costumes. For example, in the hunting scene, which is traditionally the first scene in *Cinderella*, removing most of the red from that scene will allow you to use Hunting Pink in the costumes, enabling the characters to stand out from their environment. A limited colour range, predominantly two or three colours, will allow more choice of colour within the costumes and props. For example, setting a pantomime in the winter and using whites, blues, and silvers can be very effective.

When choosing your colour palette it is crucial that you consider the lighting and how the choices of colour might either assist or hinder the lighting designer. It is quite usual for moods and colours to switch mid-scene, particularly going into musical numbers. Careful choices can allow for these dramatic colour changes in the lighting.

Leaving space for the action

Pantomime's boisterous comedy and the dance numbers will need a considerable amount of open stage space, so any scenes that have full company, chases or choreographed musical numbers will need to be given as much of the full stage as possible. It is also crucial that you allow useful acting space in front of your furthest downstage cloth. Frontcloth scenes are usually there to cover major scene changes happening behind. This might include more than just a couple of the main story characters and could involve your chorus in a musical number. Allow a minimum of 2 metres (6ft 6in) between the front edge of the stage and the cloth.

Spectacular moments

It is now when discussions concerning the spectacular moments within the pantomime should happen, so that the technical and cost issues are considered alongside the design of the rest of the set. These staging moments give the creative team an opportunity to add their original twists that make their particular pantomime unique, such as an interesting variation on what Cinderella's carriage might be. These impressive stage effects will be discussed more fully in Chapter 10.

Planning out the position of scenes onstage

To plan out the scenes, use the ground plan of the theatre (which should already have the positions of the portals marked onto it from preparing the model of the 'open stage') and begin to map out where and how each of the scenes will function within the space available. Do this before considering what you are designing within those scenes. It is crucial that you can make the pantomime work practically within the stage space, knowing when you might need to insert a frontcloth scene to cover a scene change.

Begin looking at the action within the script or story outline for each scene and decide how best to describe this on stage. Can the scene work with an empty stage with a flown cloth to provide the location? Or does it require more structure, such as onstage doors, windows or large scenic props (these include flown scenic flats and trucks, described later in this chapter). It is useful to go through this checklist of requirements to ascertain what is essential to the story. This will help focus your design and avoid creating too much scenery, which may either cause storage issues, lack of acting space, or stretch the budget. Remember to look at how scenes can alternate between frontcloth and full stage to allow time for scene changes!

Dealing with the practicalities of scene changes this early in the design process is quite unique to pantomime but it is necessary to make the production flow from one scene to the next. It is the 'kiss of death' if you let the pace drop due to an

Drafting out the positions of the scenes on the groundplan for Aladdin.

overcomplicated scene change or have to add extra dialogue to cover that change.

Remember in all this planning to keep reminding yourself about lighting. It is very easy to get carried away and forget that some bars need to be prioritized for lighting (at least four onstage, spaced evenly, usually just behind each of the portals). It is no good having the most beautifully conceived scenery if it cannot be lit creatively.

Creative solutions to challenging scenes or storylines

It is at this early design stage that the designer can act as a visual dramaturg. This is a term that

The outside toilet, designed to get around a difficult scene change in Cinderella.

describes an attitude change within the role of the designer. It suggests that the designer can use their skills and expertise in storytelling, research and spatial awareness, to not only support but to add their voice to the decisions concerning the creation of the narrative, and in the case of new writing for pantomime, helping to sculpt the shape and storyline. The designer can make creative suggestions for changes and interesting alternatives to the some of the order, or content of the scenes. In some instances the designer might have the initial idea for an approach to an important moment in the pantomime (Cinderella's carriage, the beanstalk, etc.) which could influence the rest of the development of the pantomime.

In *Cinderella* the design led to changes within the narrative of one of the scenes. The original first draft of the script called for a repeat of the kitchen of Hardup Hall in Act 2, but a section of the ballroom (added in the interval) had to remain upstage, so there was not enough room to bring that entire set back on stage again. Instead, the idea of shifting the scene to the garden of Hardup Hall was suggested. The script called for Cinderella to be locked in a kitchen cupboard by the Ugly Sisters to stop her trying on the glass slipper. This was substituted with her being locked in an outside toilet attached to the wall of the Hall. This created one of the memorable moments in the pantomime. The Fairy Godmother waved her wand, and in a flash the walls of the toilet fell away, revealing Cinderella sitting on the 'throne', turning a possible problem into a magical moment. This is one demonstration of how effective collaboration between design and writing can produce great visual scenarios.

THE DIFFERENT SCENIC ELEMENTS USED IN PANTOMIME

The following are explanations of the different types of scenic elements that might be utilized in the designing of a pantomime. Throughout are visual examples of scenery, props and furniture from several productions that show the traditional and, at times, more creative solutions. This will

Frontcloth design for Dick Whittington and his Cat.

The backcloth for Jack and the Beanstalk, *showing how the onstage scene was extended into the distance to Fairy Bo Peep's windmill (Jack played by Ricardo Coke-Thomas; lighting design by John Harris).*

give a good understanding of terms and equipment before going on to the design itself.

Cloths

Cloths can be flown in by different methods, depending on the facilities of the theatre. They can be flown in on counterweight bars if the theatre has a fly-tower. If not then they could be mounted onto rollers suspended and hidden upstage of one or more of the portals. Then via a pulley system they can be raised and lowered from the wings. Instead of rollers, cloths can be tripled like a roman blind, which is a simpler method and construction than the roller, but will give quite a jerky movement as they come in and go out.

Frontcloth or showcloth

This is the first part of the set that the audience sees when they enter the auditorium, and establishes the style and humour for the rest of the show. This cloth is quite often used in other scenes, so it can either suggest a road or 'in-between' place that is a link to other full stage scenes, or it can be a more generic cloth that portrays the theme or title of the pantomime rather than a place.

Backcloth

This is the farthest upstage cloth. It can be as simple as a plain-coloured cyclorama, lit to change moods or atmosphere during the scenes, or a painted sky cloth as a background for the majority of full stage scenes. It can be used in conjunction with a scenic ground row (explained further down this list), or it can be a full landscape design that links with the onstage scenery and extends the sense of perspective into the distance.

Cut cloths

Cut cloths have either sections of them cut away to allow access to other items of set, or are the cloth portals that frame the scenes and mask the wing space. Sometimes if these are intricate then net is added to the back of the cloth to keep the cloth from flopping or folding in on itself. The edges may also need reinforcing to help keep their shape.

Star cloth

These are useful for complete changes of time of day or location. Used upstage they can be an alternative to the cyclorama or sky cloth and transform scenes to a starlit night. They are great when used in the finale and with the addition of falling snow can make it all look very Christmassy.

Shark's-tooth gauze

This is the type of gauze that appears solid when lit

The fit-up of **Cinderella** *at Watford Palace Theatre showing the set of forest cut cloths.*

An upstage star cloth in the finale from **Dick Whittington** *(Fairy Bow Bells played by Liza Pulman; lighting design by John Harris).*

from the front and transparent when lit from behind. A black shark's-tooth gauze set in front of a white cyclorama can help make the transitions from night to day (and vice-versa) more effective. Shark's-tooth gauzes can be also be fully painted and when lit from the front will look the same as the other flown cloths, but when lit from behind can reveal another scene or characters. This can be a useful way of doing instant transformations such as the pumpkin turning into the coach in *Cinderella*.

A gauzed frontcloth will allow a cross-fade from the end of the prologue, slowly illuminating the opening scene with full company going into a big musical number. A gauze used in this manner will need a black cloth set directly behind it, which is flown out just prior to the lighting change. This is because any light upstage of the gauze will make it transparent and you will need some light to be able to position scenery and performers prior to revealing the scene.

Flats

Flown flats
Flown flats are a great way of creating backdrops to scenes that might require working architectural details. These could be complete ornate façades with windows and doors in them. Built-in entrances (either doors or openings) will allow more interaction between the characters and the set and may give a good central entrance.

Flown flats can have extra depth added in the form of second fascias to create more of a sense of dimension, or have working cupboards, shelves or furniture fixed to them, thus avoiding having to set these items up separately. It is important to make sure that with these more dimensional flats, there is enough room in the 'flies' for them.

French braced flats
These are the flats that can be set on stage for scenes and are supported by a triangular-shaped brace or braces and stage weights at the back of the flat.

Ground rows
The low level cut-out flattage that is positioned just downstage of the backcloth to add a sense of depth and distance such as rolling hills, mountain ranges or town silhouettes. It also has a practical purpose: to mask the bank of lighting on the stage floor which is there to illuminate the bottom section of the backcloth.

Headers
Horizontal pieces of scenery that close off the top

The flown flat for Neptune's Palace in **Dick Whittington and his Cat,** *showing a central entrance and windows that allow views of characters entering upstage (actors: Peter Holdway and Jeff Nicholson; lighting design by John Harris).*

127

A ground row including a windmill with moving sails in a scene from Puss in Boots *at Theatre Royal, Bury St Edmunds. Also shown are the village houses created as sliders at either side of the stage (actors: Eddie Elliott, Kerry George and Bradley Clarkson; design by Will Hargreaves; photography by Keith Mindham).*

of the set. They can be made as hard flats or cloths and stretch the full width of the stage. Practically, they are there to mask the lighting rig and in the case of the front header, the theatre iron.

Sliders

Pieces of set that are suspended on tracks to run across the stage behind one or more of the portals. When not part of the scene they are pulled offstage and should sit hidden behind the legs of the portal. If the tracking has pulleys and cables added the slider flats can be moved on and off from an operating point in the wings. This way the flats can appear to move of their own accord. Sliders can be a really good way of creating a set when there are

no flying facilities at a venue.

Songsheet

The songsheet should be created to fit with the rest of the design. This could mean linking it to the character leading the singing, or possibly a theme within the story. Having fun with silly objects and different shapes can enable the songsheet to be humorous in its own right. The background colours should be pastel shades with the lettering in black for clarity. The best way to accurately recreate a typeface is to print the text onto acetate, and then project the image and trace around the lettering. The most important thing is legibility. The size and style of typeface must be carefully

Sliders as the set

At the Theatre Royal in Bury St Edmunds we wanted to do a pantomime and create sets that were in keeping with the historic Georgian theatre by using drawn perspective and sliders. We now have a kit of a series of four portals, and behind each one you can have three or four large sliders that can independently slide in and out and create a good sense of perspective for the scenes. What is also lovely is to actually see the transformations between scenes, and even though the sliders are manually operated, this process can appear quite magical to the audience.

An advantage of sliders is that you can have them as complex as you want to make them, even with gauzed panels, doors and windows. The upstage ones can also offer the opportunity to create a strong central entrance either through doors inset into the sliders or by leaving a gap between two. If you shape both edges they can become an item of centre-stage scenery which the actors can fully interact with.

Because you can easily change the combination and position of these sliders on stage, by mixing them up, you can change the perspective or focus of a scene. For example, in the village the houses could move with the actors as they stroll to a different part of town.

Will Hargreaves: set and costume designer

chosen to make sure that it can be read from the back of the auditorium. The songsheet is usually made up as a flown flat (usually on one of the first bars upstage of the proscenium). With theatres that do not have flying facilities then the songsheet can be set up on an easel or painted onto a banner that is held aloft by two of the chorus.

Trucks

These move large pieces of scenery on and off stage, and can be manual or motorized. The set items are mounted onto a base that has wheels or castors set into them. The wheels can either be multi-directional or single direction. Single-

The model of Cinderella, *showing its different fascias and locations in and around Hardup Hall.*

direction wheels are useful when a truck has to move on and off in the same manner each time. Multi-directional wheels are useful where trucks need to be shifted around to hit their marks. If trucks are housed in offstage storage areas then the multi-directional wheels will make it easier to manoeuvre them around in the wings.

Trucks can be as simple as single items of flattage or as complex as whole room sets or even houses. In Cinderella, Hardup Hall was designed as a large truck set upstage at the opening of the show, hidden by part of the forest. The trees moved aside (sliders) as the Hall trucked downstage (manually pushed from behind). In its centre stage position it could be opened up like a dolls' house to reveal Cinderella's kitchen, and then closed and spun through 180 degrees to reveal the ugly sisters' boudoir.

Multi-level trucks

Trucks can create entire scenes that have more than one level. These larger trucks will require a steel framework to support the weight of actors on top of them. When designing these it is important to get guidance as to how much structural support will be required – with careful planning this support can be hidden by scenery.

In *Aladdin*, the 'cave of wonders' was designed

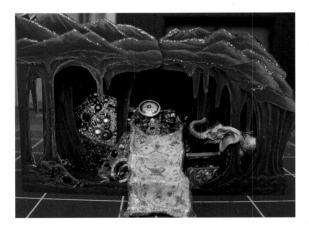

The model of the two trucks that surrounded the flying carpet, creating the 'cave of wonders' for Aladdin.

as two trucks that were set together surrounding the mechanism for the flying carpet. The entrance to the cave was through a hole on top of the trucks. Aladdin lowered himself into the cave, landing on the flying carpet. When Abanazar locked him in, a stone slid across the top of the truck and covered the hole. Aladdin escaped when the Genie granted his wish and the two cave trucks split and moved off into the wings, leaving Aladdin free to fly off on the magic carpet. (How this flying carpet was created is discussed in detail in Chapter 10.)

Stopping the movement of trucks

Once in position, trucks will have to be fixed to stop any movement. One method is the use of drop bolts into the stage floor. However, theatres may not want large holes drilled into the stage and these holes can cause problems with narrow heels getting stuck in them, for example. They can also be difficult to locate in quick changes and dim lighting. The preferred option is to fix mechanical brakes to the sides of the trucks. These are raised to lock the truck in position (lifting the truck off its wheels), then released to lower them down onto the wheels to move the trucks around. However, these are large and the mechanisms to operate them are visible on the outside edges of the truck, so they will need small items of set designed to mask them.

DESIGNING THE SCENERY

In pantomime the set is allowed to tell the story. In other genres, scenery is there to support and enhance the action, never to dominate or draw attention to itself. It is the exact opposite in pantomime! The set is there to impress and can add its own narrative to the story through its imagery and wit.

Traditionally, the design of the scenery is predominantly based on painted cloths that provide the backgrounds to each of the scenes, and allow for multiple locations. Scene transitions are achieved by flying one cloth out to reveal another scene preset behind it. In today's theatre this can appear an old-fashioned style of staging. So, should this remain the tradition, or is it time to

Two scenes in the model of Jack and the Beanstalk *showing the combination of three-dimensional painted scenery and cloths. It also shows how the same truck can be opened up for inside the cottage.*

search for alternatives?

To move away from cloths to more structural settings certainly allows the characters to interact with their space more fully, but in doing this are we then changing the quality of the production to something that is no longer seen by the audience as pantomime?

The answer lies somewhere between the two. It can work well to have some three-dimensional structures for scenes, creating real stage depth, but if these structures become too sculptural they jar with the artificiality of the pantomime world. What tends to succeed are three-dimensional structures that have painted flat fascias, similar to the fold-out sections in a children's pop-up book.

Humour and kitsch within the design

It is really important to inject moments of wit and quirkiness into the design of sets and costumes. This humour can, at times, manifest itself as kitsch or camp. These are two words that are difficult to define, yet they are often used to describe the quality of pantomime. What starts out as children's storybook imagery is subverted by the injection of irony, bad taste, saucy jokes or double entendres, both in the text and directly painted onto the scenery. This can even be seen within the style of drawing, stance, shape, or the combination of colours.

Forest camp

In *Cinderella*, the trees in the enchanted forest had to move magically about the stage. This led to the decision to give all these trees characters faces, to humanize them, so that the movement made more sense. My intention was that these should appear childlike, but on reflection, having drawn them, and looked at the arrangement of branches, roots, facial expressions and hair/leaves, they had taken on a more camp persona.

Keith Orton

The model box showing the trees in the enchanted forest from Cinderella.

131

The frontcloth for Jack and the Beanstalk showing the visual jokes that were created from the town name 'Windy Bottoms', a gift for any would-be punster.

Sharing a sense of humour

Only in pantomime does the audience relish the retelling of old jokes and still find them hilarious. There is great scope to immortalize these old jokes on the scenery and in the costumes. When the humour is at its most successful it is difficult to see any difference between the style of humour in the script and in the set and costumes: they gel perfectly. Look for those opportunities to build upon the comedy that is begun in the script, finding ways to add those visual twists.

It can be really engaging when there are little details on the set for young and old to discover. Hidden jokes and characters on the cloths and set pieces can help the young ones stay engaged. This is particularly useful on the showcloth/frontcloth because the audience sits in front of it for long periods of time before the show, and then again in the interval.

Releasing your imagination

This is the one theatre genre where the designer needs to let their imagination run wild and forget the need to make everything logical. Pantomime is by its nature illogical so don't let your staging fight with the absurdity of this form of storytelling. Of course, it is important to do the visual research to help come up with the initial ideas, but this research is a stepping-off point into an imaginary world created by the writer and designer.

Always have a sketch book to hand, as you never know when you will come across something that adds another possibility to the comedy or locations. This can be something you see in other forms of entertainment or current news which suddenly has a comic potential within the design. The audience will have seen some of the same events and news items over the past year, so mocking these within the sets and costumes make an instant connection.

Choosing your design method

The design can commence through sketching ideas on paper or in a workbook, or through working with shapes and colours directly in the model box (the scale version of the empty theatre, including the floor and portals). Whatever method you use should build upon what has already been conceived in the design of the 'open stage'.

If your choice is sketching out ideas first, try periodically photocopying these sketches and placing them directly into the model; this can then lead on to further sketches or new possibilities. It is by placing the sketch in the model that a truer sense of scale and depth can be explored. If it remains in the sketchbook there is always the

clear photographs of all your experimentation so that you can share these with the writer/director. Where possible, play with these shapes together in the model box, exploring the set and script spatially.

It is during this time that characters' entrances and exits can become plotted into the script. This will entail discovering the geography of the location. For example, where does upstage take you in your pantomime world? If exiting stage right or left where does this go? It is useful to know now where characters' homes or rooms are located

Initial ideas for the cave scene in Aladdin, *then placing and developing the sketch idea into 3D within the model.*

difficult transition between the two-dimensional drawing and the three-dimensional final model.

The design can also be developed entirely within the model box. Begin by adding rough shapes that represent the scenic elements. You can then move these shapes around to see how they interact with each other and how, through line and shape, they draw focus or provide locations or entrances within a scene. This can be a really effective method when developing the design alongside the script.

Once a suitable arrangement has been established, you can begin to draw details onto the shapes and slowly develop the final design. Take

Taking initial white card shapes and developing them into the final design model for Jack and the Beanstalk. *Some scenic elements were reversed and the large cottage truck was removed to allow the full company space to do their opening number.*

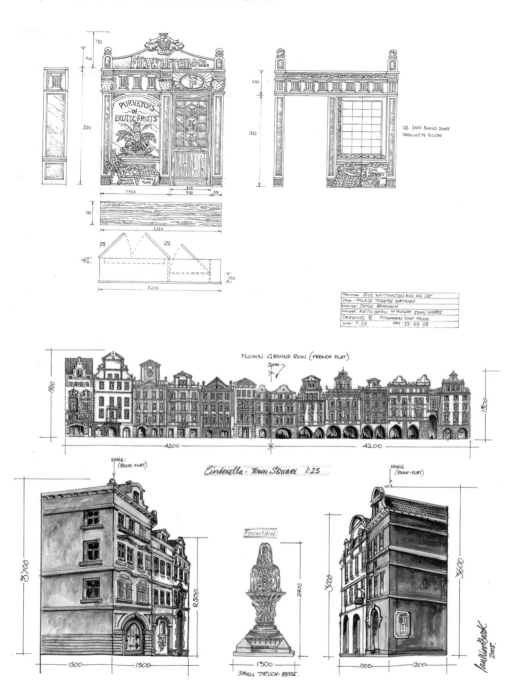

The technical drawing for the shop truck from Dick Whittington and his Cat *(prior to colouring), and a coloured version created by Ian Westbrook for* Cinderella, *showing the similarity in the use of the technical drawings as artwork for the constructors and scenic artists.*

offstage, as this might eventually manifest itself in onstage signage or designated entrances between specific portals.

When developing the design and script for *Jack and the Beanstalk* the quick sketch model was a means of deciding how the transitions occurred between the scenes, the best use of space, and logical flow for the story. For example, in the opening scene our first thoughts included the cottage for Trott's Dairy mounted on a truck as part of the town square to help establish the dame's presence in the town right at the beginning of the show. However, the moment we saw the shape in the model we knew it was too dominant and would block too much of the space, limiting the choreography for the opening number. So it was removed and brought on as part of the subsequent scene.

This meant writing a different first entrance for Dame Trott, and a frontcloth scene to cover the subsequent scene change. The design of the dairy also had to change to become a complete truck that would fit between the portals when wheeled on from the wings during a scene change, rather than being preset for the opening of the show.

Making the technical drawing part of the design process

Because of the hand-drawn nature of pantomime scenery, the final drawings can feed into the technical drawings required by the makers. When preparing the final designs, produce a line drawing first, before adding colour. This line drawing can then become the basis of the front, side and plan elevations on the technical drawing.

Create these line drawings directly onto technical drawing paper, or as separate artwork that can be scanned and dropped into a drawing programme such as Sketch-up, CAD, or Vectorworks. These line drawings can then simply have the dimensions added to prepare them for the scenery build. They can also be used by the scenic artist for drawing up the design, as it will be easier than working from the full-colour model. They will quite often use projection as a means of quickly drawing up the scenery; with the black-and-white line drawing this process is made easier.

To create the final artwork use inks or watercolour onto a photocopy or print-out, or by using a paint programme on screen. This coloured artwork can then be used to create the final model by taking full-colour drawings and scanning or photocopying them. These copies can then be mounted onto board and cut out and assembled. The scale of the final model can be decided at this point. It is simple to reduce a 1:25 scale drawing to 1:50 scale without losing any of the detail that was in the original. (A 1:50 scale model can be easier to transport from place to place when meeting with the writer or director.)

Having separate full-colour technical drawings also means that the final model can remain intact throughout the lengthy construction and painting processes, leaving the model in good condition for presenting to the company on the first day of rehearsals (quite often months after its initial construction).

PROPS

All props for pantomime need to match with the drawn quality of the set. Props purchased from retail outlets will have to be adapted and painted to bring them in line. Pantomime props are usually larger than life-size to emphasize the comedy, and because of their over-sized nature, they are often made from lightweight materials such as Plastazote foam to make them not only easier to manage, but soft enough to be able to hit other characters with.

Characters' hand props

Certain pantomime characters will require specific props. For example, the fairy will require her wings and wand. In *Cinderella* the ugly sisters may have their prop beauty products, and Dick Whittington must have his red-and-white spotted handkerchief attached to a stick for him to carry over his shoulder.

Because they all need designing, it is a great opportunity to look at how these traditional items can be given a new twist. In our version of *Cinderella*, the Fairy Godmother worked for 'Fairy Godmothers R Us' so we gave her a fairy mobile

The Fairy Godmother with her traditional wand and non-traditional mobile phone (played by Gina Murray; photography by Manuel Harlan).

phone, and her wings were packed away in a little rucksack that she could pop out on cue.

Some of the requests for props can be very bizarre. In our version of *Cinderella* the script called for a kitchen blender that the wicked stepmother could use to shred Cinderella's invitation. Not just that, but then the fairy Godmother could reverse the process and magically blend it back together. This was achieved through a false section fitted into the back of the blender with a mirror in front so that the invitation was hidden away. The base of the blender had a battery fan and small pieces of paper were blown around at the flick of a switch to appear as if shredding the invitation. The switch was thrown again (this time by the Fairy

Godmother) to reverse the process and then once the blender had stopped, the Fairy Godmother could simply remove the complete invitation from its mirrored section.

Large-scale props

As well the hand props, pantomimes can throw up some interesting challenges for large-scale props that are integral to the storytelling. Some provide hiding places for characters such as chests and cupboards; others provide the means for characters' entrances. It is really important to make sure that these large props can be manipulated easily by the actors and that their actions are planned carefully to make sure that they function in the way that the script and the design requires, get on and off stage efficiently and have the space in the wings for storage.

Prop transport

Large prop vehicles such as cars, small boats and the like can be designed and made to clip onto the performer's waist allowing free movement around the stage. The design will need to include a skirt that reaches the floor to hide the performer's feet. For large items a frame with wheels can be added to take the weight away from the performer. In *Dick Whittington* at Oldham Coliseum this method was

Dick Turpin and Bess from Dick Whittington *at Oldham Coliseum as a large inhabited costume/truck designed by Celia Perkins.*

used to create Dick Turpin's horse, Black Bess, with the addition of false legs to create the illusion of the performer sitting astride the horse.

FURNITURE

Furniture in pantomime is usually kept to a minimum as it can restrict the action of a scene or slow down the scene changes between different locations. Some of the furniture that might have been dressing in a scene is instead painted onto the backcloth or flattage. Any furniture put on stage will have a definite purpose within the narrative of the scene.

Furniture should always have the same aesthetic as the set, therefore it is impossible to put real/bought items of furniture on stage without giving them the panto treatment. The furniture is quite often required to withstand a lot of misuse including being stood on, so it will need to be designed and built to withstand these rigours.

However, it should also be built so that it is light enough be set onstage quickly, possibly with castors or wheels on larger items. Small items of furniture such as stools and chairs will be moved around by the actors so should be lightweight and have handholds where necessary.

In some cases the furniture can establish the entire location of a scene and be the only major item of scenery. In *Jack and the Beanstalk*, the Giant's castle interior was created by using a huge armchair and standard lamp. This was designed to fit with the concept of the castle being built from the clouds but was also to help make the scene look more comforting and less scary for the little ones in the audience. It was made as a complete piece and mounted onto a truck base for ease of movement and storage. The wooden structure was covered in wadding and topped off with stretch Lycra, stapled in to create the cloud-like appearance. It was then painted into to get the finished effect.

Furniture for Jack and the Beanstalk *with rustic stools that were sturdy and had overhanging lids for ease of lifting and positioning (actors: Christopher Robert, Andrea Miller, Richard Ashton, Dale Superville; lighting design by John Harris).*

The cloud chair and lamp from Jack and the Beanstalk *(actors: Richard Ashton, Alice Jackson and Martine Burt; chair and lamp designed by Simon Wells).*

9 LIGHTING, MUSIC AND DANCE

The contribution of lighting and music/sound and choreography should never be underestimated. They add their own dimensions to the narrative and performance. They have their own qualities and needs that should be acknowledged, in some form, right at the beginning of the creative process. This might be in the way that the writer/director and the set and costume designer include discussions about the qualities of the music/dance and lighting as the show is being conceived.

When working professionally it is extremely unlikely that the lighting designer, musical director, or the choreographer will be employed at the same time as the set and costume designer, but just keeping them informed through emailed images and getting initial conversations going can create a better working relationship, and a much more cohesive finished production.

LIGHTING

Considering light as a means of painting the scenes

Lighting needs to work with the absurdity of the stories and be as quirky and dynamic as the script,

the set and the costumes. The set may use certain tones and hues that the lighting can either work with or even intentionally against. The colour palette and effects that the lighting designer uses is much closer to rock-and-roll lighting, with brazen use of colour. It should in no way appear naturalistic. It is also very unlikely that the colour palette for a certain scene will even remain constant. As soon as a musical number is introduced the quality and style of lighting will shift to working with the music more than describing the scene. Once the number is over, it might revert back to its previous state, or the musical number may have left its mark and changed the mood of the ensuing scene.

The characters' entrances can be announced through the use of light. This is most obvious with the baddie, who is traditionally picked out in green to signify his evilness; but even the heroine might need a complete shift of colour to bathe her in a rosy romantic glow, and the dame may have lighting chosen to enhance a particularly outrageous frock.

In the technical rehearsals, adjustments to colours can be made in discussion between the lighting designer and the set and costume designer,

OPPOSITE: *A musical number from* Jack and the Beanstalk *(actors: Tania Mathurin and Dale Superville with junior chorus member Lauren McDonnell; choreography by Nikki Woollaston; lighting design by John Harris).*

Use of contrasting colours from either side of the stage to create a sinister effect for King Rat (Peter Holdway) in Dick Whittington and his Cat (lighting design by John Harris).

since certain elements painted onto the set or costume fabrics might not have the necessary impact when lit in certain colours. This will be a matter of negotiation as each designer will have reasons for wanting the space/characters to look a certain way.

Creating a sense of time and place

As several scenes are played out in front of the same painted cloth, the lighting can be crucial in establishing the time of day. This should be considered when the cloth is being designed to make sure that the colours and shadow work can help the lighting create its desired effects. If the cloth has windows or means of illumination painted onto them, then adding LED lights and even illuminated panels (gauzed and lit from behind) can create more interesting effects. If a scene takes place at night then it will inevitably be using cooler washes with strong deep blues, and scenes that take place in the baddie's hideaway may use a lot of strong greens. It is important to register these at the beginning as some detailing in

the design may get lost under certain lighting states.

Lighting and costume

Lighting should always consider the costumes. The same costume can include matt, high sheen and sequins all at the same time in a wide variety of colours, so choosing appropriate lighting colours can be tricky.

With LEDs and high-powered batteries it is now possible to build lighting directly into the structure of the costumes. LEDs can be used to create twinkling effects and larger light packs can be added to illuminate entire sections of costume if the fabrics used are translucent.

Understanding the genre

For a lighting designer it is very important to understand the style of the particular pantomime. If it is very traditional with numerous cloths and portals then the lighting has to reflect this. Use of lighting batons and footlights will be essential to make sure that the cloths look their best and

New ways of achieving fully lit backcloths and cycloramas

A new method of creating backcloths in theatres is with something called LED Arrays: a wall of LED modules arranged in a grid format using red, green and blue (RGB) LED lights. This whole thing is set approximately 300mm (1 ft) behind a backcloth or cyclorama, usually with a reflector cloth behind and where possible, the back of the cloth needs to be reflective white. With this setup you can address the function in several ways:

- You can use the colours either individually or mixed to seamlessly colour a cyclorama.
- You can address the system as if it was a picture. You can take a jpg image of say a sunset and then feed that into the lighting desk, in various ways, to programme the LED Arrays to duplicate a low resolution version of the sunset across an entire white cyclorama.
- You can also create a jpg image of a painted backcloth and do the same process, so that you can then intensify a section of the cloth such as the sky or illuminate windows without having to use additional lights or light boxes.

This technology is constantly upgrading and has the advantage of saving precious lighting rig space. It also uses less power.

Nick Moran: lighting designer

Illuminated lantern frock from the finale of Aladdin *(actors: Peter Shorey and David Webber; lighting design by John Harris; photography by Manuel Harlan).*

Understanding what it is to be seven years old

You must consider the age of your audience and work with the idea of lighting the show for a seven-year-old. You look at things differently when you are that age. Your colour spectrum is different, and your attention span is shorter. There is no point in spending hours lighting beautiful moments that will go unnoticed by your audience. For them it is much more about use of colour and movement and the lighting needs to make much bigger statements. You have to remember if you are seven you are swept away by things and you just buy into what is being presented to you. In lighting, as in any of the other creative elements, you don't need to over-produce it because children pick up visuals quickly, and are soon ready for the next trick.

John Harris: lighting designer

crease-free. This is particularly important when using cloths that are not brand new and have been taken out of storage, or hired. No matter how much spraying and stretching they undergo, it will be impossible to remove all the creases, so the lighting needs to help eliminate them.

Due to the number of scenes and consequently the flying of scenery and cloths, there will always be a limited number of onstage bars available for lighting. If you are lucky the set designer will have given consideration early enough in the process and left at least four onstage bars, usually directly behind each portal and one to light the backcloth.

Part of the set for Sleeping Beauty *(Qdos Entertainment) showing a complete palette of different lighting effects (designed by Ian Westbrook; lighting design by Ben Cracknell).*

Layering with lighting

With the improvement of equipment in recent years, the palette of effects that can be achieved relatively easily has increased. With the inclusion of projection and more sophisticated gobos (cut-outs placed directly in front of the light), scenes can have numerous layers within the lighting states, combined with 'built-in practicals' (lights embedded in the set) and projections all working together. Only in pantomime could this amount of brazen mixing be acceptable.

Follow spots

Follow spots are used to isolate or highlight moments, or track characters through musical numbers. You can also focus in on characters and create poignant or romantic moments by shrinking the spot down so that the light reduces to just the face or faces and then shrinks to blackout. The follow spots will need their own plotting list, prepared during the rehearsals in discussion with the director.

A follow spot is used for the character of Tinkerbell in *Peter Pan*. Here a pinpoint of light is flicked around the stage to show the flight of the fairy. With the accompaniment of appropriate sound/voice the audience are swept into believing this light is the fairy. When Tinkerbell takes poison instead of Peter and nearly dies, the careful flickering of the light, done sensitively, can give the illusion of the fairy's life ebbing away. Only with the audience eagerly pledging their belief in fairies does she come back to life and the light flicker back to full brightness.

Blackouts

Creatively it is important to decide whether the pantomime should have blackouts or bleed-throughs/cross-fades for scene changes. This will depend very much on the design of the scenery. Some set designs will require the blackout to make the transitions between the scenes cleaner, to avoid seeing large pieces of set or furniture being moved into place by the stage crew. However, there will be some instances where painted gauzes have been created (instead of cloths) to allow the action to bleed through from one scene to the next.

Afraid of the dark

It is important to understand the effect a blackout can have on the younger members of your audience. Young children will get scared by being plunged suddenly into darkness, especially if this happens right at the beginning of the show. So avoid having a blackout for at least ten minutes whilst they get used to being in the semi-darkness of the auditorium. It can be difficult to calm children if they are screaming because they are scared. Some even have to be taken out and could miss the entire show.

John Harris: lighting designer

Follow spots used to isolate Fairy Bow Bells (Liza Pulman) as she casts her spell, whilst Tommy the Cat and Dick Whittington (Dale Superville and Tom Bradley) listen out for the bells that call them back to London (lighting design by John Harris).

143

It is also a question of preference: some productions consider it is part of the concept of pantomime to see the cloth fly out, in full view, revealing the next scene; others prefer to have a blackout while the cloth flies out, followed by the lights fading up to reveal the next scene.

Bringing the design out into the auditorium

With the introduction of moving lights and projections the design can now be thrust out from the stage into the auditorium. Special gobos, such as glass slippers and pumpkins for *Cinderella*, or spinning wheels for *Sleeping Beauty*, can be created and projected over the theatre auditorium and boxes. These could be static or animated at certain times, such as the overture. It gets the young audiences really excited when the lights move off the stage illuminating them and swirling around to the music.

Ultra-violet 'ballets'

Special effects scenes can be done under ultra-violet light: certain objects and creatures are picked out using colours that fluoresce under UV light while the rest of the stage and parts of the actors that you don't want to be visible are blacked out. For the best effect, use UV tubes rather than UV guns as the coverage is greater and they warm up quicker. UV can be a great way of staging a magical moment or spell, or can create a spooky effect for a 'ghost scene'.

For total illusion it should be done in a black box or against black drapes, without any other scenery,

 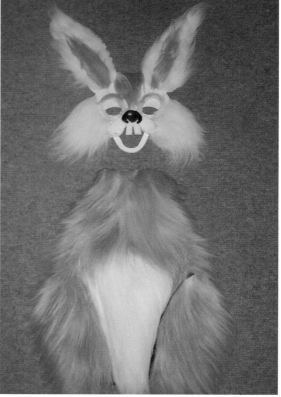

Design for scary bunnies (mask, bib and gloves) in the UV scene in the enchanted forest in Cinderella.
Here the junior chorus could hop around with the rest of their bodies blacked out.

A scene from a workshop at Central School of Speech and Drama where we did a pumpkin transformation using white mice puppets that sailed down on umbrellas, which became the carriage wheels. Details were picked out in clear UV paint and the scene was lit with both UV and stage lighting to begin with, and then switched to UV to transform the pumpkin into the coach, which was then drawn offstage.

because any other colour on the set will inevitably show up in the UV light and spoil the illusion. If the pantomime portals must remain then the action should be centred between the portals against a black backcloth.

The performers/puppeteers should be shrouded in black, including their hands and faces. This is usually done with a black body stocking that includes a hood, black gloves and black organza to cover the faces, but still allow vision.

In most cases it is impossible to mix normally lit characters and UV characters unless the distance between them is vast, as light will bounce, spill and overpower the UV.

These 'ballets' can be difficult to choreograph as it is important to always keep the cut-out, puppet or character facing the light, because as soon as shadow is cast the illusion disappears. However, it

is worth all the effort as a good UV ballet can be enchanting, and the youngsters adore it.

Being practical

With pantomime having such an established structure, the lighting designer can save a lot of time by creating a standard rig that can almost be transposed to any pantomime. This is made easier nowadays, with the use of moving lights (not necessarily used for their mobility but because you can change colours quickly and easily and use the same lights for numerous scenes). This is not 'cheating' as it will buy important time during the plotting and technical rehearsals. Lighting a pantomime can be as complex as lighting a musical, but the lighting designer will only get a fraction of the time usually allocated to a musical, so this short-cut can be hugely beneficial.

145

MUSIC

Music has a huge impact on the storytelling. A song can quickly change the mood or tell the audience more about a character than several lines of dialogue. In pantomime the hero and heroine/love interest fall instantly in love, which is made much more palatable by how you underscore that moment and then follow it with them bursting into song. When first thinking of the ideas and structure for the story the writer may already have had ideas for certain songs that progress the narrative (*see* Chapter 3). Music will help build up tension for the scary moments and punctuate the funny bits.

Choosing the right music

Music is a great way of bringing generations together. Pantomime can employ different types of music, such as Music Hall, and Gilbert and Sullivan songs if you are trying to create an extremely traditional pantomime, or pop music for more modern takes. When using pop music, try and choose songs from different decades – some recent ones, some that will appeal to the parents, and some for the grandparents.

Well-known songs work best, and using an older song that's been covered more recently can work really well. For instance in recent years Abba songs have gone down well as the older audience know the music, and the younger ones have

Liza Pulman as Fairy Bow Bells doing her patter song, with backing by King Rat and the 'captured' King Neptune (Peter Holdway and Jeff Nicholson) in Dick Whittington and his Cat *(musical supervisor and arranger: John Rigby).*

watched the film *Mamma Mia*.

But, as in most things to do with pantomime, you can have a complete mix of traditional and modern and these choices might depend as much on the quality of the actor's singing voices as suitability for a particular scene or moment between characters.

In our version of *Dick Whittington and his Cat* the pantomime was set in 1908 so we chose to use some of the old songs to help locate that time period, and with the casting of Liza Pulman from Fascinating Aida as Fairy Bow Bells we were able to include a Gilbert and Sullivan patter song that fitted with the time period and the excellent quality of her voice. But in the same pantomime we had a selection of pop songs ranging from the 1960s through to the present day. This mix had no real logic other than fitting with the narrative and mood of particular moments in the pantomime.

Don't get behind the times

Keeping up to date with chart music is important, so check out what kids are listening to currently. Be aware that young kids have favourite films, TV shows and adverts that can be parodied. Even if these are only used as quick snippets, they can have an impact, and cause much hilarity amongst

Oliver Tompsett as Prince Charming 'rocking' in his ballad 'Accidentally in Love' in Cinderella *at Watford Palace Theatre (musical director: Matt Smith).*

> **Building the music from the set pieces**
>
> I definitely begin with the big set pieces, such as the flying carpet or the growing of the beanstalk and how those big moments will be staged. It is also useful to consider major movements of the set such as revolves or trap doors that might have an impact on the direction the music might go. I believe that these major set pieces set the tone for the whole pantomime, since everything builds up to, or is a consequence of these moments. For me this applies if choosing existing songs or composing new music.
>
> *Zara Nunn: musical director/composer*

the young ones.

The hero and heroine will have a ballad or duet, not only to show their love for each other, but also to add variety to the music used. Choosing the right ballad can be tricky and the length will need to be kept short to make sure the little ones don't get bored, and to prevent the song from holding up the story.

To get around this in *Cinderella* we used 'Accidentally in Love' by Counting Crows (it had just been used in *Shrek*). Here Prince Charming sang of his instant love for Cinderella. This gave a fantastic upbeat moment in the show and was a perfect fit in terms of the story.

Bringing all the different songs together

Such a contrasting mix of pop and traditional songs will, in some way, need pulling together. This can be done in the way that the musical director does the arrangements. Tempos and instruments can be changed from the original and brought in line with the style and orchestration of each particular pantomime.

Size of band

This can depend on available space and budget as much as what best suits the show artistically. Once the style and quality of a particular pantomime has been established then the selection of music to

147

accompany this can be considered. For example, you might want to vary the type of musical instruments if your pantomime is set in a particular time period or geographical place. This might, however, be managed through the use of a keyboard and synthesizer rather than accommodating a specific instrument.

You could have a band of one if the musical director plays both piano keyboard and synthesizer and can multi-task. However, the more usual set-up is three musicians (piano/keyboards, bass guitar and drums). This will give the band the scope to do rock and roll as well as the ballads and more traditional songs.

A live band is preferable, as so much of the 'stingers' (band sounds coming at the end of a joke or sequence) and underscoring of the scenes might need to adapt to what is happening on stage. Stumbles and difficulty with scene changes can be quickly covered by the band, who can pad out musical phrases or add punctuating sounds to the end of ad-lib gags or prat falls.

The depth of sound can be increased by creating click tracks for the big musical numbers. These are pre-recorded tracks that can add to the orchestration for certain songs or dance numbers and are played alongside the live band.

King Neptune and Sarah the Cook sing 'Dead Ringer for Love' in Dick Whittington and his Cat *(actors: Jeff Nicholson and Howard Coggins; musical supervisor and arranger: John Rigby; lighting design by John Harris).*

Where to put the band

Traditionally the band is in the orchestra pit, which is situated between the stage and the audience. In this position they are often required to interject during the show. The musical director is quite often referred to by name, and might be asked to give his or her opinion on some of the discursive moments with the audience, such as the songsheet. There is no need to hide them away, as the audience enjoys seeing their interaction with the show.

The band can be placed on stage if there is an appropriate space and if it is part of the design concept, but the musical director must have good visibility at all times. So if the band is upstage of the actors, a monitor will need to be located front of house so that the company can see the musical director.

It is also quite usual for the band to be costumed, to link them with the story. This might be as simple as appropriate headgear, particularly if the musicians are in an orchestra pit.

Musical arrangements

In most pantomimes the music consists of arrangements of existing songs, dances and jingles rather than original work. So the creative input is in how these are edited and developed to fit with the onstage action and provide the underscoring between scenes. The musical arranger/musical director will work from a playlist that is usually partly formed within the script. But there is always at least one number that is elusive. It is quite usual to have brainstorming sessions between the director/writer, designer and choreographer during the early days of rehearsals to make last-minute selections.

For example, the duet between King Neptune and the dame in *Dick Whittington and his Cat* came out of a decision that the original choice, 'You're The One That I Want' from *Grease*, was too obvious; and the actor playing Neptune had a huge voice. After much discussion, the musical supervisor had a 'eureka' moment and put on a CD of Meatloaf's 'Dead Ringer for Love' and the die was cast. This was perfect as it gave scope for both showing off Neptune's voice and adding humour

---

Making full use of a song

When I first get the script, and go through the songs listed, I am already considering which songs will be the key to certain characters or dramatic moments. For example, we re-wrote the words to Abba's 'Money, Money, Money' for the dame in *Aladdin*. Then every time she made an entrance that song was used in the underscoring to tell the audience she was about to enter.

Songs can also be reprised in the underscoring of scene change music to continue the mood created during a scene. Or, by using a song from the next scene, the audience is given an indication of what is to come.

Zara Nunn: musical director/composer

---

from the dame. This number became an absolute showstopper!

Music choices may also be made around scene structure and character. Many of the main characters will expect to have a song or a musical number in which they are highlighted (often a solo or duet). If this is omitted, and they do not have a moment in the 'spotlight', the actors concerned may feel put out. These numbers can be chosen to give more depth to individual character or characters rather than stop the progress of the story.

Parody in music

Using classic and instantly recognizable music at dramatic moments of the pantomime can be a way diffusing tension and adding to the humour. Audiences love to see the witty way scenes and their music are juxtaposed. In *Jack and the Beanstalk* the Giant's castle needed to be a scary place for the characters but not too scary for youngsters in the audience. A giant chair and standard lamp needed to truck down stage as the scene opened. This movement took a few moments to complete, so we needed music to cover this. The musical director came up with the theme tune from 'Mastermind' which because of its association with a black leather chair gave a humorous parallel with our cloud one, which the audience got straight away.

Silly Billy and Jack discovering the Giant's chair (actors: Dale Superville and Ricardo Coke-Thomas).

Composing original music

Where productions have more time and money, some choose to stage pantomimes with a score of completely new music. This has the advantage of being written alongside the script so will be a perfect fit with the narrative, but will have the disadvantage of not having the instant recognition with the audiences. However, a way around this is to create music and songs that parody existing work, so that although the audience may not know the particular song, they can see what it is echoing, and as a result, humour can be gained from this association.

Where new music can really work is in the dance numbers, and by bringing existing songs together in a medley for such things as the overture, opening number, or the finale. With dance numbers the director, choreographer and musical director can work together to create a number that has the right tempo for the dance and fits with the narrative. It is unlikely that this collaboration can be more than a discussion on the phone or via email, but with new technology, sharing music with others can be much quicker

and easier.

When linking existing songs and new writing it can be useful to begin with the script and produce a new musical theme created directly from the scenario or part of the dialogue. Then existing songs can be chosen to work alongside this newly composed theme.

When writing new songs, be aware that they will need to be upbeat and catchy – perhaps with daft, easily-heard lyrics. This is particularly important if you are writing the song for the songsheet, where the audience needs to pick up the tune and words after just one hearing.

Amplifying the voices

Preferably, all the cast's voices will be used in creating the harmonies, so they all will need radio mics to get the balance right. When using radio mics, the packs that house them will have to be

Different starting points

When working on the medley for the finale of *Dick Whittington* the script indicated that the medley had to flow out of the dialogue and that the singing needed to sound like it was coming from the Bells of London. So I had the whole melody begin with bell chimes: a two-beat melody over a three-beat rhythm which gave it a weird feel, but if you listened carefully you could get a sense of the bells. From that I developed a complete ten-part melody using the voices to create the chiming bells.

In contrast, when working on the end of Act 1 in *Aladdin*, there was no script at the time of composing. All I knew was that a flying carpet would lift off at the end of the number. So I began by writing the lyrics to get a sense of the narrative. It took time to find an angle, but then I stumbled across a tag line which was, 'Rise, Prince Aladdin' (linking the two ideas of the investiture of a Prince with the motion of the carpet) and from that I was able to write the whole number. The script leading into that number was then written once the song was complete.

Zara Nunn: musical director/composer

allowed for in the making of the costumes. There is nothing worse than seeing a lump (mic pack) in an otherwise sleek dress or tight breeches.

Managing rehearsal time

The pre-production time with the band will be brief. They usually arrive in the theatre the day before the technical rehearsals and will have that morning to make sure they can play the music and then it is straight into a sound check with actors singing through the numbers, sharing that time between the musical director and the sound operator.

This will also mean that all the orchestrations with accompanying click tracks will have to be completed well before the technical rehearsals begin, as this portion of music will be difficult to adapt or change. Numbers that are played entirely by the band live can have more flexibility.

Sound effects

This is a highly creative process in pantomime. The vast majority of sound effects have a heightened sense of reality to fit with the rest of the show. Where else can you be asked to create the magical squelch and explosion of a pumpkin growing into a coach, or the sound of a baking cake? Sound effects can be wonderful additions to slapstick moments, for example a long whistle sound as paint is emptied from a great height, and to add the essential element of comedy to a fight scene – a duck quack sound every time the baddie is hit on the bottom. The right sound can make the whole audience giggle, and give the scene a cartoon-like quality.

Recorded sounds are created and played through the sound desk. Some sound effects can be played live by the band either through the synthesizer or using duck whistles, car horns and other strange percussion instruments.

Getting performing rights

Remember that all recorded and published music is protected by the Performing Rights Society (PRS) and you need to get their permission to use any published song, for which you may have to pay. However, turn-of-the century Music Hall songs will be out of copyright so may not cost you anything to use. It is worth noting that it can be difficult and expensive to get the rights to use music from Disney films.

DANCE

Movement and dance has always been an integral part of pantomime. Going back to its origins of commedia dell'arte and through the introduction of the Harlequinade, the characters have always expressed part of the story through dance and movement. Today's pantomime has such an emphasis on visual puns and songs to accompany the action that the role of the choreographer is a crucial one.

In pantomime the cast may have been chosen more for their acting, singing and comedy, and may not be natural dancers. So in order to gauge the cast's potential it is important that the choreographer is involved in the casting process, to check for an appropriate standard of movement, but also to look for those people who might be able to tackle more complex choreography. This can be done by teaching a short routine within the auditions, and checking their CVs for what they have done in the past.

Choreography for pantomime does not have to be technically complex but the company should be confident enough to sell the dance with self-assurance.

Dance troupes

Some pantomimes use separate local dance troupes that are rehearsed and choreographed by their dance teachers and then slotted into the show during the rehearsal weeks (in the evenings). Sometimes these dancers and their routines are kept completely separate and they don't appear at any other point in the show.

Some theatres will mix a young dance troupe with adult dancers. Here the choreographer will work with the adults during the day and then add the youngsters in the early evening (after school). Dances might be choreographed and then taught to the children by their dance teacher for several weeks prior to the theatre's rehearsals, particularly

The junior chorus doing a short scene in Jack and the Beanstalk *(actors: Tania Mathurin and Dale Superville).*

if the dances are complex.

It is nice where possible to integrate the junior chorus (dancers) into the scenes in the pantomime, working with the principal characters, some even having the occasional line of dialogue. This might mean the children are cast as much for their acting as their dance moves, so it may take them longer to learn the dance steps. In this way the junior chorus is integral to the show and their family and friends get more of a buzz from their fuller involvement.

Working with the designer

As mentioned previously it is important that the designer communicates with the choreographer as soon as possible. The choreographer will need to know how much stage has been allocated for a particular scene, where that scene is taking place, whether there are stairs, raised levels or other scenic elements that can be integrated into the choreography. For example in our production of *Cinderella* the opening number took place in the enchanted forest where the trees moved around the stage on sliders. In conversation with the director and choreographer the trees were also

The junior chorus as sea creatures in a musical number with Neptune's daughter played by Alice Jackson in Dick Whittington and his Cat *(choreography by Nikki Woollaston; lighting design by John Harris).*

The company of Cinderella *in full flow in the clever ballroom scene, which combined modern with period moves (actors: Stephen Boswell, Oliver Tompsett, Debra Michaels, Andrew Bolton, Madeline Appiah and Daniel Crowder; choreography by Nikki Woolaston; lighting design by John Harris).*

choreographed into the opening number, moving with the actors and the music.

They will also need to see the costume designs to check where movement might be restricted or where gussets need to be added for better flexibility. Then there is the question of length: do they have long trains, capes or tails that might get in the way? If there are costumes that are based on creatures or objects will any of these lend themselves to particular moves?

In *Dick Whittington and his Cat* the scene that opened Act 2 was an underwater ballet with Neptune's daughter 'Persil' and the junior chorus dressed as jellyfish and sea urchins. The costumes where discussed at design stage, and again part way through their construction to see how they would move in response to the dance as it was being conceived and rehearsed.

Where clothing is quirky or oversized it might be

It's a kind of magic

For the ballroom scene in *Cinderella*, I had an idea of mixing period dance and modern steps. There is a scene in the film *A Knight's Tale* where they do this – they start dancing to classical music and it merges and becomes rock dancing to David Bowie! I asked Nikki Woollaston, the choreographer, if we could use this kind of mix. She came up with a minuet, which was started by the King, that gradually evolved into a rock party led by the Prince. By the end of the song the characters were bumping hips in time to Joan Jett's 'I Love Rock and Roll'. It allowed us to mess around with period, encouraging audience participation with an over-the-head hand clap, and lots of silly comic moves too, interspersed with the more regal 'minuet' moves.

Nikki also managed, through lots of swirling movement, to make the expansive ballroom look jam-packed without the need for a large chorus. It was a wonderful number that culminated in a slower romantic section, which is needed when the Prince and Cinderella meet and fall in love. It was an example of dance itself telling a lot of the story.

Joyce Branagh

---

emphasized in the dance or movement routines that are created. The choreographer might also ask for certain complex costumes in rehearsals, or rehearsal costumes that approximate the shape and scale. It is important that the scene designs and costume designs are clearly displayed in the rehearsal room so that the choreographer can refer to them and make sure nothing gets overlooked.

With the animal friends/skin parts it is important that movement is discussed thoroughly; it is as good to discover what a costume can't do as much as what it can. With something like the pantomime cow, this should be in rehearsals from day one as it is only through playing with the costume with the performers in it that the full potential can be found. Also, the more the actor/actors wear and play in the animal costume the more effective their animalistic movement becomes.

Working with the director

The choreographer and director usually form a close bond in the rehearsals, and usually help each other with the blocking and movement particularly with specific pantomime gags, such as 'behind you' moments and the comic character's slapstick routines and prat falls, where the movement has to be precise to create the gag.

The choreographer might also be asked to work on audience participation moves that are then taught to the audience by certain characters as part of the plot. They may also create moves to go with the songsheet song which are silly and easy to pick up, so that the audience can throw themselves into them instantly.

Parodying famous dances

Like all creative aspects of pantomime the use of parody is a winner. With so many dance shows now on television there is a much greater interest, and more informed understanding of dance. There are several dance sequences from films that have become iconic, so pantomime choreography is foolish not to tap into this in some way. The body lift in *Dirty Dancing*, or fairground hustle in *Grease*, are examples of this.

Finale musical number 'Diamonds Are A Girl's Best Friend' with Christopher Robert as the Dame (accompanied by: Dale Superville, Alice Jackson, Tania Mathurin, Richard Ashton, Peter Holdway, Martine Burt and Natasha Cox; choreography by Nikki Woollaston).

In our version of *Jack and the Beanstalk,* Joyce wanted to use 'Diamonds Are a Girl's Best Friend' from the film *Gentlemen Prefer Blondes,* with the dame dressed as a bizarre Marilyn Monroe. The costume and dance moves were parodies of the film original.

A good choreographer is always up with latest dances/TV shows/dance videos that the young people are getting into, and is able to make reference to these new crazes in their choreography. They will also have knowledge of classical dance movements such as ballet, tap and ballroom, which will be recognized by the older members of the audiences, because, although it is good to keep up to date, it is also good that the routines have more than a small touch of nostalgia.

10 MAKING THE MAGIC HAPPEN

Back in the nineteenth century when pantomime was much more epic in its scale and number of performances, there were always the major 'coup de théâtre' moments that required huge casts and complex moving scenery. And today's audiences still enjoy a little 'spectacle'.

When to put the spectacle into the pantomime

Each pantomime should be structured in a way that builds to a spectacular moment or moments. How these are incorporated into the pantomime will depend very much on the story you are telling. A lot of the pantomimes have very obvious moments, such as the growing of the beanstalk in *Jack and the Beanstalk* or the sinking of the ship in *Dick Whittington*. The staging of these can dictate when the interval occurs, as the spectacle usually requires large scenic elements. Staging a spectacular moment before an interval break will avoid creating a long scene change afterwards, and leave your audience with something to talk about during the interval.

Spectacles used once or twice, and contrasting with simpler/quieter moments, can be stunning. However, if a show is crammed with them, this might appear a visual feast, but will in fact be less effective, with not enough build-up and anticipation of the coming effect.

Concealing the magic

An important aspect of these spectacles is fooling the audience. To keep the 'magic', the audience should be unable to work out how it was done. The transformation of Cinderella using a double (discussed in Chapter 6) is an established trick that the adults may know immediately, but should leave the young children spellbound. With the flying carpet in *Aladdin* there is an opportunity to fool all ages and have it fly around the stage without ever showing its mechanics (this is discussed in more detail later in this chapter).

Your script and direction can help make magical moments more successful. An exciting dialogue interchange happening downstage can deter most of the audience from realizing that upstage a switch is happening, or that a pyrotechnic is being put in place.

Design taking the lead

These moments are by their nature a mix of the visual and the technical, and only once the idea has been drafted out and its technical

OPPOSITE: *Richard Ashton as the Giant in* Jack and the Beanstalk *(costume made by John Brooking and Dawn Evans).*

specifications fully appreciated, can it successfully be included in the script. This is why it is important to discuss the spectacles right at the beginning of the process. Creating these may have more unusual demands (such as flying, fountains and pyrotechnics), which have health and safety implications and may need the expertise of outside personnel or companies.

If scripted without consideration of its design and realization it might prove difficult to achieve and lead to re-writes or disappointment. It is important to avoid times when the narrative of the scene is not realized in the action of the spectacle; an example would be where the beanstalk looks fantastic but the structure, due to its design and realization, limits how much Jack can climb it, when the script specifically dictates that this is what Jack needs to do.

Knowing how it will function

With pantomime it is important that the creative team understands how an effect might be achieved. This does not mean that they have to have an engineering background but they should always take advice from other professionals to make sure that the realization is as simple and reliable as possible. This would also include where you want to fly actors around the stage as this will require a professional flying company to advise, give training, or be present in the theatre when the systems are being operated. This can be extremely costly and, if on a tight budget, you may need to find a more creative solution.

Simple but magical

Magical moments don't necessarily need large budgets. Sometimes the simplest trick can appear totally magical. In fact, one of the easiest ways of adding magic is the use of glitter on the set and in the costumes. Having this element of sparkle, with appropriate lighting will transform flat colours and surfaces and immediately transport the audience into the magical world of pantomime.

On painted cloths and cut cloths it will twinkle with the slightest movement. Use glitter on the edges of objects where the light would catch it in the same way as you would usually highlight with white paint. Scenic glitter comes in a wide range of colours and sizes. Wherever possible apply glitter to cloths once they are hung in the theatre as a lot

Scenic artists Julian Day and Fiona Stewart applying glitter to a showcloth designed by Terry Parsons.

Glitter by the bucket

I always have a showcloth and use glitter by the bucket to decorate it. I see it every year: the kids light up the moment they walk in. They audibly gasp and it is not because it is a fabulous design, it is because it is something that is uniquely pantomime. It is like entering a Christmas grotto. They can go to a lot of shows where they walk in to see the front tabs, but with panto – I love it – from the second they go through the door they can tell what sort of evening it is going to be, and that is why I have never done a pantomime without a highly glittered showcloth.

Terry Parsons: set and costume designer

of the glitter can be lost in transit from the scenic workshop.

Another simple effect is the use of a mirror ball. These are easy to obtain and rig but still have that magical quality when cross-lit, providing little flecks of mirrored light that swirl across the set and auditorium.

MAKING THE MAGIC A REALITY

The next part of this chapter is dedicated to explaining some of the classic magical moments within pantomimes. These will be primarily based on our own experiences and the solutions that we discovered, together with additional examples from the work of the designers Will Hargreaves, Terry Parsons, Celia Perkins and Ian Westbrook.

It is worth remembering how much the audiences buy into the onstage silliness, so pantomime tricks and spectacles can be low key and still appeal. A flying carpet scene done in UV, with Aladdin wearing a UV painted cardboard carpet suspended at the waist can be as equally enjoyable as a fully mechanized version.

Flying carpet

Aladdin's magic carpet can be done in a variety of ways to give the illusion of flying. Here we describe how to create a flying carpet that can physically lift actors and fly them around the stage with no visible means of support. This particular method calls for major structural support and mechanisms to give the illusion of effortless flying.

It is based on a see-saw type motion. The carpet

The showcloth from a production of Cinderella *designed by Terry Parsons for First Family Entertainment. It shows the level of detail in the painting and glittering required by his design style.*

itself is mounted onto a pivot arm made from a triangular box section or H frame (preferably aluminium to keep the weight down). Whichever way, the arm needs to be rigid so there is no give lengthwise, as this would apply extra pressure on the pivot point and the operation end of the arm. At the operation end there needs to be a counterweight cage mounted as far back as possible; this is loaded with weights to counterbalance the weight of the carpet (actors included); it should be fractionally lighter, so that the 'loaded' carpet will always want to sit on the stage rather than in its up position. If weighted correctly the carpet can be operated from the rear, by two stage hands, without them having to strain. This will enable a much more fluid flying motion.

It is very important to have a well-manufactured pivot and bearing plate as this is where the pressure falls and the motion needs to be a smooth and free as possible.

You will also need to build in a locking system so that the arm can be locked off with the carpet in its down position (minus the actors), otherwise the sheer weight of the counterweight cage will force the carpet to its highest point. Once the actors have got into position on the carpet, then this locking can be released and the carpet is ready to fly. It is also imperative to lock it off at the end of the scene,

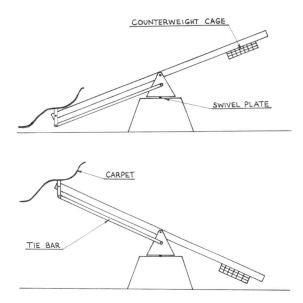

Diagram of the flying carpet showing the tie bar that keeps the angle of the carpet constant, together with a picture of the part-finished carpet in the workshop.

before the actors get off the carpet, to avoid the counterweight cage forcing the arm to plummet to the stage, possibly endangering the operators and the actors.

To achieve a sense of floating, a tie bar can be fixed and pivoted under the main arm to keep the carpet parallel to the stage as it 'flies' (see diagram of the structure).

The carpet itself was made from a small gauge bar frame that was clad with wadding and fibre

The flying carpet from Aladdin *showing the use of side lighting to avoid lighting the underside and the mechanism (actors: Stefan Butler and Rachel Grimshaw; lighting design by John Harris; photography by Manuel Harlan).*

glass to get the shape of the carpet. It was then painted and decorated with heavy gold fringing.

To meet with health and safety regulations and to make the actors feel more secure we gave them lap restraints to buckle themselves onto the carpet. We used airplane lap restraints for this and decorated them appropriately. This was anticipated early enough to build a scene into the script that had the Genie donning various disguises (as airplane staff) to deliver a comedy safety check, whilst the actors fastened themselves in; then the carpet was ready for take-off.

The entire mechanism below the carpet is invisible as it is blacked out with velour fabric and lit from the side, only illuminating the performer's faces on the carpet. When the carpet took off headlights dropped down from underneath, giving it a 'Chitty Chitty Bang Bang' quality. The headlights shone beams of light into the auditorium, disguising the front edge where the mechanism joined the carpet.

Cinderella's carriage

The appearance of the pumpkin carriage comes at the culmination of the Fairy Godmother's spell and transports Cinderella off to the ball. This is usually staged at the end of Act 1 to avoid a complicated scene change part way through an act.

This carriage must look totally magical. Formed

Two extremes

The following are two descriptions of carriages that were designed and made for specific productions: one was for an arts centre and the other for a large-scale commercial pantomime.

When designing *Cinderella*, our pumpkin carriage was not 3D as I couldn't afford it, nor did I have the knowledge to build it myself. So, I went for a 2D cut-out outlined in UV paint with fairy lights running around the outside of it. Although this was done as much for cost as anything, it was just as magical and fitted in with the rest of the design. It got an initial giggle from the audiences as it was wheeled on, but that was only because they found it silly and not because it looked out of place.

Simon Wells: set and costume designer

In one of our productions of *Cinderella* the carriage is replaced by an automated winged horse (Pegasus). It was not that deep, only about 1 metre (3ft 3in), but it had huge articulated wings which were on cantilevers, a sort of cross between Muppet technology and Thunderbirds. Pegasus rises out of the stage and Cinderella mounts the horse and is flown off to the ball (into the wings).

Ian Westbrook: designer from 3D Creations

Production shot of Cinderella's carriage at the Guildhall School of Music and Drama. The three-dimensional coach had 1,000 LED lights and fully functioning wheels (constructed by students at GSMD; designed and photographed by Philip Engleheart).

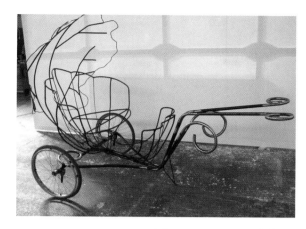 

The construction of the rickshaw-style carriage (minus glitter) for Cinderella.

from a garden pumpkin its shape and design often reflects this. The pumpkin carriage can be as simple as a cut-out mounted on a truck base or as complex as a complete horse-drawn carriage; the choice will be dependent on budget and storage/animal welfare. You can also decide if you want the carriage to enter downstage so that Cinderella climbs aboard or if it is preset upstage and revealed through a shark's-tooth gauze. Both can be magical through the generous use of glitter and fairy-lights/LEDs – it is important that the whole carriage sparkles. If your stage is small then revealing a preset carriage might be your best option. Remember it will only need to begin moving off to the ball as the scene finishes, so may not need to exit into the wings.

For our production of *Cinderella* we had a small carriage similar to a rickshaw, having three wheels (two bicycle wheels and a small pivot wheel). It was designed to be lightweight and easy to manoeuvre around the stage, because we had decided that we wanted it drawn by the junior chorus dressed as mice. The scripted indicated the need for full 360-degree movement, so it was built to almost turn on the spot.

Taking to the high seas

Several pantomimes have ships as an integral part of their stories: these include *Dick Whittington, Peter Pan, Robinson Crusoe* and *Sinbad the Sailor*.

How these are achieved onstage will depend very much upon how the scene is written. Scenes set on deck can utilize the open stage with flown masts and accompanied by a raised level or truck upstage (the wheel-house or poop deck). If the stage has traps then you can even have entrances from the hold of the ship. With this option shipwrecking is best done with sound effects and possible bits of 'falling' scenery. Even buckets of water could be thrown over the actors from the wings (providing the stage floor is designed to allow for this). The swaying movement of the ship can be done by the actors staggering from port to starboard. This 'on deck' method is best where the scenes are lengthy, with various sections of dialogue and musical numbers. However, if the scene on board ship is short – for example, the ship leaves the dockside and is almost immediately sunk – then the option to do a three-dimensional version can be both silly and clever.

In *Dick Whittington and his Cat* we wanted to create a large three-dimensional paddle steamer that could quite literally steam around the stage with the cast in it. The construction was timber frame, clad with skin plywood. It was designed to be trundled around by four of the cast with one 'steering' it from a small wheel house. The steam came from a mini smoke machine inserted in the funnel, which could be operated from the wheel house. The base of the ship was open so that the

The paddle-steamer for Dick Whittington and his Cat *being constructed in the workshop at Watford Palace Theatre.*

The finished paddle-steamer showing the ship split in two. The stern slots in behind the curved shape of paddlewheel (actors: Howard Coggins, Liza Pulman, Sia Kiwa, Dale Superville and Tom Bradley; lighting design by John Harris; photography by Manuel Harlan).

cast could shuffle it around using their feet.

The sinking of the ship was achieved when the two baddies (in a rubber dinghy) planted a bomb on the side of the paddle-steamer. A metal plate was inset into the side of the ship, and the bomb had a large magnet on its reverse to make it fix on

Captain Hook's ship in *Peter Pan*

In a version of *Peter Pan*, for Qdos Entertainment, the designer Ian Westbrook was tasked with creating a 27-foot ship that could sail out of port. A galleon of this size would be too big to fit in the wing space of most theatres, so Ian Westbrook came up with the following solution.

I started with the black-and-white line drawings; I did the side, bow, and stern views and designed it in four sections. We then went straight from the drawings into the build. It was all on trucks that could be quickly toggled together. So, as the ship came on, you saw the bow and first mid-section appear as the other two were being wheeled into position and clamped on. Then, when it needed to come offstage the first two sections were unclamped and removed the moment they got into the wings, followed by the dismantling of the back two. That way you could get a 27-foot ship into a wing space only 12 feet wide!

Ian Westbrook: designer

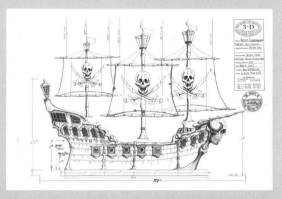

Design drawing for Captain Hook's ship showing the three flown sails and the body of the ship, which splits into four trucks.

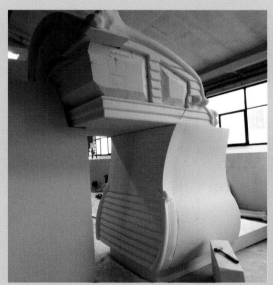

The pirate ship in the workshop under construction, then set onstage showing the depth of the ship and the eyes illuminated in the skull figurehead (design by Ian Westbrook; built by 3D Creations).

contact. To create the explosion the ship then sailed around so that the bomb side was facing upstage. A pyro was positioned upstage centre of the boat and on cue was fired and created a mushroom cloud of smoke giving the impression that the bomb had gone off.

The ship then split in two (by uncoupling pin-hinges). As the band struck up the opening chords of 'Breaking up is hard to do' the cast pulled the ship into two parts and they swirled around the stage singing as the ship sank and the curtain fell.

Trojan camel

For *Aladdin* at Watford Palace Theatre, we created a Trojan camel that was used to smuggle Aladdin, Widow Twankey and Ping and Pong (the Emperor's policemen) into Abanazar's Palace to rescue the Princess. The initial idea for this came from Joe Graham, the writer, but then the way in which all four characters could fit and provide moments of comedy was developed more fully through the design.

In the scene, the camel was delivered as a present, and once alone on stage the head swivelled and eyes flashed to signal all was clear, then the two humps opened up and the heads of Ping and Pong popped up to look around. They then got out and moved to the back of the camel.

The Trojan camel arrives onstage (Genie played by Howard Coggins; camel designed and built by Mike Bell).

They lifted the tail to release the back end of the camel, which folded down to create a ramp and Widow Twankey slid out of the camel's backside dressed as a palm tree.

This was constructed as a steel frame, which was then clad in skin plywood. The upstage side of the camel was completely open (the camel was only ever seen side on) and had perching points inside for the four actors. They also manually operated the head movements and the flashing eyes.

The Giant

In the original telling of the story, the Giant is portrayed as someone who is defeated by Jack and killed when the beanstalk is chopped down. Morally, this is tricky, as in essence he is chasing Jack who is stealing his property. So when staging *Jack and the Beanstalk* for today's audiences you either have to keep the Giant alive or make him a totally evil 'trespasser-eating Giant', which may prove a little too scary for the younger ones.

Animated puppet

Using a large animated puppet removes some anxiety about killing the Giant (by de-humanizing it). The other strength is being able to play with scale in relation to the human characters. However, one of its downsides is that it can appear clumsy, and it can be difficult to build expressions into the face without spending vast amounts of time and money. This type of giant can be hired in when there are not the resources or the time to create your own. But with its lack of movement and expression it is more likely to be used sparingly in the story. If the narrative requires more onstage time then using an actor might be a better option.

Actor as the Giant

When casting an actor as the Giant their height and build is an obvious essential. The taller the actor the more realistically you can clothe their body to make them look like a giant. Even so, their height will need extending using stacked heels or stilts. Stilts can be created with false boots built into the base to extend their height. An extension of 60cm (2ft) should still allow the performer to

Giant in Jack and the Beanstalk *at the Theatre Royal, Bury St Edmunds (with actors Lotte Gilmore, Dennis Herdman, Jonathan Eiø; designed by Will Hargreaves; photography by Keith Mindham).*

Richard Ashton as the Giant and Ricardo Coke-Thomas as Jack in Jack and the Beanstalk. *This Giant needed to appear as a real person because of the surprise revelation that he was Jack's long-lost father, allowing us to parody the similar revelation between Darth Vader and Luke Skywalker in the* Star Wars *trilogy (lighting design by John Harris).*

Two heads are better than one

The best giant I ever did was played by two actors playing a giant that had two heads and three legs (two legs strapped together, like in a three-legged race). This was a concept that was taken and developed directly from an idea by the writer. It was terrific: they could play scenes on their own with the two heads talking to each other. And because it was this strange concoction it still looked really weird and impressive without the body and the heads looking out of scale. In effect we were going wider rather than taller. But, best of all, the audiences really loved it.

Terry Parsons: set and costume designer

walk around without needing the support of a pole or stick. This increases the leg length but not the torso, so the waist will need artificially lowering to make the Giant appear more in proportion. With the use of padded shoulders and clothing the Giant's frame can be given extra bulk.

A false head placed over the performer's can create a better-scaled head, and even though this can be animated, using expensive automated parts, it will cease to appear human and become puppet-like. But, by adding a large wig and beard to the human head, the face can appear larger and you have the advantage of full facial expressions from the actor.

Frontcloth scene at Bury St Edmunds where the fairy uses puppets to tell the story of Jack chopping down the beanstalk and killing the Giant. The full-scale scene was then set behind the frontcloth (Fairy played by Annie Wensak with dancers Polly Pateman, Jessica Eden and Christy Kemp; design by Will Hargreaves; photography by Keith Mindham).

Jack's beanstalk

This famous pantomime vegetable is an important feature within *Jack and the Beanstalk;* it provides the magical link between the village and the Giant's castle in cloudland. You could choose to create a beanstalk that grows before the audience's eyes, or it could be covered by a frontcloth scene, whilst the beanstalk is erected upstage of the cloth.

Growing before your very eyes

This method has the advantage of continuing the action of the scene but invariably will create a beanstalk that is difficult to climb without some fairly complex technical support. The growth can be achieved in several ways, such as a fly line attached to a soft structured beanstalk. This can be set inside a piece of stage set or within a trap in the stage floor. The beanstalk is then pulled slowly up and it unfurls as it grows.

You can also do this as a UV scene with the beanstalk being a flat canvas with a rope ladder attached to the back for Jack to climb. The canvas is laid out on the stage floor or fixed on a roller and is raised using pulley lines. This is particularly popular with theatres that have no flying facility.

Revealed in all its glory

By having a frontcloth scene to cover the change a much more structural beanstalk can be flown in or positioned using a truck, or – in the example discussed here – a combination of the two.

In our version of *Jack and the Beanstalk,* we had

Getting the beanstalk to grow and making it strong enough to climb

We created a beanstalk that grew out of the trap in the stage floor. This started as a small shoot attached to a line that could be pulled out of the open trap through dry ice as it began to grow. The last 6 feet of the beanstalk was solid and equal to the depth of the understage. This was finally winched up to stage level and gave a section of the beanstalk that Jack could actually climb very effectively as the curtain came down on the end of the Act.

Will Hargreaves: set and costume designer

Another method is a fully inflatable beanstalk which is made out of rip-stock nylon and is inflated with the use of a massive fan hidden beneath the stage or behind a ground row. This is probably the most costly method because the actor playing Jack has to mime the climbing as he is actually hoisted out on a yo-yo fly line, which needs the technical support of a professional flying company. However, the effect can be truly impressive as it grows so quickly and it will gyrate as the air fills the contours of the stalk. A tether line is used to keep it on track.

Ian Westbrook: designer

A telescopic beanstalk that was raised by using a hydraulic ram under the stage, with a fine 2mm Kevlar wire at the top to guide its growth. An actor could climb up to the top using a hidden safety line within the beanstalk trunk (designed and constructed by Ian Westbrook).

decided that the beanstalk would talk, which immediately gave it a personality. During its development it changed sex from male to female (due to casting) and developed a cod French accent.

It was designed and built in two parts: a truck, the main structure of the stalk; and then a flown flat which had three-dimensional stalks and leaves

The beanstalk for Jack and the Beanstalk, *showing the steel framework of the truck, the beginning of the poly-carving, and the beanstalk part coloured with its leaves being selected, made by prop makers June Douglas and Mike Bell (pictured).*

designed to fit onto the top of the truck and extend the beanstalk right up into the flies.

The truck was structurally built as a steel framework with poles jutting out at carefully selected positions for the attachment of leaves and to provide the rungs for climbing. It was then clad in polystyrene and carved to created the stalks and the outline of the face. The eyes, eyelids and lips were made to be manipulated from behind through the window of the cottage. This was then foam-coated (a white polymer that seals the polystyrene and creates a good surface for painting) before being given its final colouring. The leaves were made from Plastazote and spray-painted to match the rest of the stalk.

With this type of structure Jack was able to climb 2 metres (7 feet) up the stalk before the frontcloth flew in to denote the end of the Act.

Pyrotechnics

Pyrotechnics are firework charges electronically activated from the wings. There is a wide range of different types, from sparkle to smoke and explosions. All have their place in the pantomime 'portfolio', so it is a question of suitability and which can be operated safely in your performance space. Pyros can be costly: remember that the number required has to include tests of the equipment, technical and dress rehearsals, as well as the full run of performances. In small-scale venues even a small explosive might be too loud for the cast and the audience and break accepted noise levels.

Pyrotechnics are synonymous with pantomime. It is probably the only traditional theatre genre where this is so. Other than that, it is only concerts, events and TV entertainment shows where they are used. The good fairy's entrance will almost

Bringing together pyrotechnics and water

In a production called *Bollywood Steps*, an outdoor spectacular was created on a stepped stage, with spectacular lighting, pyrotechnics and water effects all going on at the same time. The things that we had to carefully consider were the fall-out from the pyros and the water fountains, the risk of burning dancers and equipment, and how to control noise.

Although not pantomime, this is a good example of the issues that had to be taken into account when dealing with electrics and water simultaneously, which have parallels with usage in pantomime.

We used what are called 'cold fall out' pyrotechnics – these reduce the risk of fire by creating cooler sparks. On the first show we did full inductions for the dancers so they knew what to expect and then planned the firing around the performance, making sure that safe distances were observed.

We also carefully chose the pyros for their visual spectacle, rather than their loudness, to make sure that we were within the safe working levels for dancers and audiences.

Alastair Noonan: technical manager

Bollywood Steps, *an outdoor dance spectacular that used pyrotechnics, lighting and water effects simultaneously.*

always be accompanied by a pyrotechnic flash. The pyrotechnic pod (the box that holds the pyrotechnic charge) is either permanently set downstage or pushed into place from the wings just before the firing.

A designer and director will always want to have the pyro go off as close to the action as possible, but most will need to be a minimum of 2 metres (7 feet) from the actors and audience when they are fired.

Always purchase specific theatrical pyrotechnics from reputable retailers. These will come with clear guidelines on the safety and operation, which should be read thoroughly and adhered to. It is important that the cast are shown the effect and told the safety precautions prior to running it in the scene. The action must be carefully choreographed around the firing so everyone knows where they should be, and the operator has a clear line of vision to the pyro pod and the surrounding stage; then if an actor is too close, the firing can be aborted. This should be rehearsed fully within the technical rehearsals so that everyone is comfortable with their operation and firing.

Safety must be the main priority when dealing with pyrotechnics. Don't even consider using them unless you are confident that they can be planned for and operated within the guidelines given.

Water and fountains

One of the trickiest of all the spectacles is having moving water on stage. This is not surprising as the combination of electricity and water is never a happy mix. There are several important factors to consider before deciding to use large quantities of water on stage. However, it can look totally magical. There is something amazing about seeing rain fall or water effects happen live onstage.

The pool of youth

Designer Celia Perkins describes how she approached the creation of the 'pool of youth' in *Mother Goose* at Oldham Coliseum Theatre. A lot of what she experienced are the classic technicalities and solutions when dealing with water on stage.

> It was an interesting challenge as we wanted to create an actual waterfall!
>
> As there are weight restrictions to the stage, not only did we have to think about the weight of the scenery, we also had to bear in mind that water weighs 1 tonne per square metre. This also had implications for the health and safety of the limited number of crew available.
>
> My design consisted of raised rostra with a central waterfall, which had a hidden door in the centre, above which was a blade waterfall. Downstage of this was a raised truck with a steel punched mesh lid through which champagne

fountains appeared and which the actor could stand on. To stage left and stage right of this were two mini pools containing hazers which drifted fog down into a lower pool. Two curved treads stage left and stage right ascended to the waterfall.

> Mixing water and electricity is clearly a huge challenge! For the lighting we used a fibre-optic system. One harness up-lit the waterfall; a further fibre-optic harness was also used to light up through the champagne fountains and through the fog in the lower pool. Space had to be designed into the trucks to accommodate the LED light engine.
>
> The base of the fountain truck was made watertight with fibreglass as this was the main tank for the waterfall and fountains with a subsidiary feeder tank beneath the waterfall truck. The challenge here was to calculate the flow of the waterfall and fountains in order to have a big enough tank for the water needed. Again space was designed into the base of the rostra to accommodate the sequence pumps as we needed – one for the waterfall and one for the fountains.
>
> Water always finds a way out! Leaks were inevitable particularly at valves joining the set pieces and within the fibreglass tank. During scene changes the technical team also became plumbers as they were required to plug together water valves as well as LX cables and set pieces. An uneven stage floor affected water flow so fine adjustments needed to be made in situ. We also found that water splashed onto the stage and treads. As we had a dance routine around the set piece we were able to regulate the water flow of the cascade fountain with control valves and change the angle of the fountains, which alleviated this problem.
>
> Fountains and waterfalls are noisy so we had to be aware of what music masked the spectacle and when to regulate the water for clear vocals.

Finally, standing water will need to be changed frequently if it comes into contact with the actors or crew to avoid the possibility of passing on water-borne germs that can breed in water when left to stand in a tank or pool.

Projecting characters

Just around the corner is promised a bright enough 'video head moving light' making small-scale projection much more manoeuvrable, for example to project heads/faces or objects onto scenic elements. This could be the Genie's head onto the smoke that billows from Aladdin's lamp, or perhaps an animated version of Tinkerbell, which can flit around the stage. Also, with automated flying you could have a scenic moon tracing up and down and across the stage, link this to the lighting desk, and have an animated face projected onto it that would move in sync with it.

Nick Moran: lighting designer

SPECTACLE FOR THE TWENTY-FIRST CENTURY

Projecting into the future

With the advent of new technological breakthroughs in projection equipment some of the more static scenes in pantomime can be given a new lift. There are opportunities for projected images to become part of the narrative of scenes and even certain characters.

Some productions already use straightforward projections in the form of digital video that can be projected onto a screen or surface of the set. These might be for things such as the appearance of the Genie or Spirit of the Ring. Because this is pre-recorded it can mean that a famous person might take this role as it will be a one-off fee for the filming. Other productions use video projection to show a journey in a 'home movie' style. This was used at York Theatre Royal for a filmed scene that had Dick Turpin and Black Bess (his pantomime horse) travelling around famous sites in London, and getting on the train!

An old staging trick that has made a comeback is the use of a projected road behind a vehicle. Here the characters pretend to be driving at speed whilst the road and various objects pass behind them on a screen. With better projection equipment and programmes for creating the animation these effects can be made even more creative and exciting, and some of these are created in 3D!

Coming at you in 3D

The other 'new' toy in the technological repertoire is 3D. This is done using state-of-the-art technology to create full stage projections onto a screen. This screen is usually flown in downstage as a frontcloth scene. To get the 3D effect the audience has to put on polarized glasses, which have to be built into the story in some way.

In Qdos Entertainment's production of *Sleeping Beauty* the 3D scene was used to show the vines growing up the palace walls. This growth was accompanied by numerous creepy crawlies that would leap out of the screen at the audience, producing squeals of delight from the young children. The putting on of the glasses was covered by explaining that we all needed to protect our eyes from the powerful magic that was making the vines grow.

This effect was also used to create a new twist for the 'ghost scene'. In Act 2 the Prince and the goodies scaled the walls and arrived on a roof section of the palace. Here a ghost rises up out of a

Moving from action on stage to projection

To create the sinking of the ship in *Dick Whittington*, I would usually have to design for this, using scenic elements, but this time the action was completely conceived as 3D projection. My scale models for pantomime are always identical facsimiles of the completed set. So, the animators filmed the model and then manipulated it in their 3D programme, so that when it went from the onstage set to the projection it was seamless. It began with a gauze in front of the set with both the ship, actors and projection in sync; then the ship and actors could be faded out as the projection took over.

Terry Parsons: set and costume designer

well behind the actors who are onstage. What was really clever was that the shouts of 'it's behind you' as the ghost crept up on the actors suddenly changed to screams as the ghost shot out to hover just in front of the audience's eyes. This was an example of how the new technology can enhance an existing piece of pantomime business.

Because pantomime uses so many cloths as traditional staging, the use of the screens for projections and 3D animations feels perfectly suited, and demonstrates how pantomime can accommodate new theatre technology and spectacle whilst still maintaining its traditions.

11 CASTING, REHEARSALS AND PRODUCTION WEEK

When the design has been completed and the director and production team take the reins, this does not mean the end of the process for the development of the story and the script. There are many occasions when scenes and dialogue will have to be altered to fit with the action that is occurring in the rehearsal room. This is something that has to be carefully handled as vast amounts of work on the set and costumes will have already been completed.

This next stage will not contain exhaustive analysis on the casting and the rehearsal process, as much is similar to that for other productions; it will concentrate more on differences that exist when dealing with pantomime.

CASTING

Ideally it is good to have a mixture of performers in the cast – those who are experienced pantomime performers and those for whom this pantomime will be their first. If enlisting good experienced pantomime performers, it is advisable to start the search early. If there are particular individuals you would like to cast in the key roles (especially the dame and comic characters) it is best to offer and cast them as soon as possible, even before the

previous year's pantomime has finished. The good pantomime performers who really know their stuff are in high demand, so if you want them to be in your production you have to move fast! Often a regional theatre has an actor return year after year (as seen by the reappearance of certain actors throughout this book). This is often a big attraction for your local audience, as they get to know their favourite dame or comic. Even without celebrity status, they can become a reason that audiences re-book.

As an example of building loyalty, at York Theatre Royal, Berwick Kahler has been the pantomime dame for over thirty years and David Leonard has been the baddie for over twenty years! They have developed such a following and reputation that the theatre has been able to vary its repertoire and cover such unusual titles as *Humpty Dumpty* and *Dick Turpin*. Even with these less popular titles, they have created pantomimes that delight their audiences. So much so, they manage to produce queues down the street when the box office opens in March.

Casting process
Because there is a large amount of music in most pantomimes, it is good to have your musical

The company of Aladdin *showing their talent in singing, dancing and acting (Joanne Redman, Kieran Buckeridge, Rachel Grimshaw, David Webber, Nicola Blackman and Dale Superville; lighting design by John Harris; photography by Manuel Harlan).*

director around for most if not all of the auditions. Not everyone in the company will have beautiful voices, but there will be full company numbers that will require everyone to join in. If you want to cast a brilliant comedian who can act brilliantly and can dance like a dream but can't sing a note, it's always good to know if the musical director thinks they can work around this. Similarly if you can have the choreographer in the auditions, or at least the recalls, they can check out those with good dancing ability, and also note those who find dancing more challenging. This foreknowledge can help them when planning and structuring the larger dance numbers.

When considering who might work well in the different roles, it is also good to think about who has the stamina and personality for pantomime, and will get on and work well as part of a company.

With two shows a day – perhaps for as long as six or seven weeks, at a time when nearly everyone is feeling tired and getting winter colds – a good company, where people get on, can help a pantomime retain its sparkle. Equally, the wrong mix of people can result in a bad atmosphere backstage which can make for a miserable time, and tensions might sometimes find their way onto the stage.

Casting a young chorus

There may be a pool of young people that you can call on from a local group or youth theatre, or possibly drama and dance schools in the area. However, it is also a good idea to try and encourage young people who don't have a performance background but might get a lot from the experience. So contact the local schools and other non-performance groups to let them know about the audition days. You will almost certainly get far fewer boys attending auditions, so make a special effort to encourage boys to attend.

When casting younger people and children, try doing a workshop audition. It is the least daunting and gets the most from the youngsters you are going to see. If run well, they can be a fun way for them to spend half an hour, even if they aren't lucky enough to land a role. Auditioning around ten children at a time works best. In that half an hour you need to check several things: can they sing in tune? Can they learn dance steps? Can they act? Do they listen? And do they have the right attitude to be in a hard-working company, but to also have fun doing it?

Begin with an explanation of the story (this is a good way to research how well your 'traditional story' is known to the young people in your area). Ask lots of questions such as, 'Do you know who the baddie is in *Jack and the Beanstalk?*' and note who answers and who doesn't. Some of the more shy children may be great performers, but may just need a bit of praise and cajoling to get them to relax. Then follow this with a game or some movement which subtly merges into them doing some acting, and perhaps even learning some steps, as a group. Then listen to them sing; this can start as a whole group exercise, but you will need to listen to them individually. They need to be brave enough to do this, and hopefully through the acting and dancing in the workshop they will be

The junior chorus as the rat pack in **Dick Whittington and his Cat** *(King Rat played by Peter Holdway; lighting design by John Harris).*

179

less scared of singing in front of the other people.

For a theatre doing performances for several weeks, you will need at least two teams of young people to alternate between performances, so in effect you need double the number. We have found that two teams of six youngsters worked well. Often young people have to share their costume with an opposite in the other team, so as you cast, ideally you need to be matching up similar body heights/shapes. Get your auditionees to give their height as they arrive to aid this process. There will always be one or two fantastic performers who are much smaller or taller than the others, so exceptions can be made, but always bear in mind the impact this will have on the number of costumes that are already required.

LEADING UP TO THE FIRST DAY OF REHEARSALS

Before rehearsals begin it is important to make sure that schedules and plans for the weeks leading up to the opening of the show have been agreed with all parties involved through consultation and allowing every department the chance to put in their individual requests. This will ease the process and make sure that nothing important gets forgotten. Also, by opening up this discussion, the sharing of rehearsal and pre-production time can be considered.

The management of this process is a role usually held by the production manager, who has responsibility for managing the production team and the weeks leading up to the performance. In small-scale productions where this role is not present, responsibility is usually shared between the director and the stage manager. Either way, good communication and considered scheduling is essential to enable the show to meet its deadline.

The creative team will also need discussions with the production manager and stage management team at regular intervals in the months leading up to the start of rehearsals. The production manager in particular provides another pair of eyes examining the development of the pantomime script and design. They may spot potential difficulties or problems. Whilst this may not always be good news, it is better to know early so that alternative solutions can be found well before rehearsals start. These early meetings also give stage management a longer time to search for or begin making specific props, which might avoid frantic workloads when the rehearsals begin. You can also arrange at this stage what items of furniture, props, etc. are vital to have in rehearsals.

A hard-working and joyous time

One of the big differences with pantomimes is in the timing: everything has to be completely decided upon, designed and ready to go, way before rehearsals start, whereas in a lot of other productions there are still elements of tinkering and decisions that can be left till the rehearsal process.

Then there is the scale of it – there is always so much to do and complete to deadline, which can be quite daunting, but actually, in a nice way it is formulaic and once you acknowledge this, the task seems a lot more realistic. Not that there aren't surprises, because there are always things that you cannot predict. But as a production manager you get to know what it needs, and there is a rhythm to it which you don't get with other shows; there is something reassuring about discovering this rhythm that combats the anxiety.

In pantomime there is a sense of joy for all those involved in any way within the production. They enjoy it because the show often does big effects without the pressures that usually arise with other forms of theatre. It is often less precious and the process and production weeks feel more relaxed and joyful because it is pantomime. Everyone works really hard, and there is always a lot to do, but it feels more fulfilling because there is always quite a thrill seeing all the different elements come together. Everyone can appreciate their contribution and the effect it has on the final production.

Ali Fellows: General Manager of the Theatre Royal Stratford East

Production meetings

Production meetings will include a representative from all the theatre departments meeting with the creative team. They are held every week, usually on a regular lunchtime in the rehearsal room. This is organized and run by the production manager and can be a good opportunity for all parties to update each other on progress, possible complications, or changes that are going to impact on the production, leading into, and including, the technical rehearsals. This might include changes to the build of certain items of set or costume, which might appear small and unimportant, but can in certain cases have a huge impact on the way that a scene is being directed. Production meetings can provide a good opportunity to sort out times for fittings and inform departments of possible publicity events where costume or props might be required.

A friendly and considerate creative team is what is required for pantomime. It will be hard on everyone to get it ready, but the team should be open to changes when things get impractical or impossible to achieve. This can sometimes happen when you are trying to create complex theatrical moments, either in the rehearsal room or, in the case of stage effects, in the workshop. Luckily pantomime is the one form of theatre where if something is not quite working, then it is fairly easy to adapt or possibly make a gag out of it.

THE DESIGN PRESENTATION AND READ-THROUGH

On the first day of rehearsals it is important to make sure that the production and promotional teams have an understanding of what the show will have to offer. The read-through that the performers do, on this first day at the theatre, can be nerve-racking for them, but if it is handled in a very inclusive way then it set the tone for the weeks to come.

Adding energy to the read-through

Most rehearsal processes start with a read-through, but because the rehearsal period for pantomime can be so short, every moment counts. I therefore always do what I call a 'standing up read-through'. Everyone who needs to see the

Keith Orton presenting his designs for **Dick Whittington,** *with the costume designs and scenic storyboard on the wall behind.*

read-through (and this can be stage management, wardrobe, marketing, etc.) sits in a semi-circle and the actors read out the play – doing a rough version of their entrances and exits. This can be very daunting for your cast on their first day, so you may want to pre-warn them.

The advantages are many: it is easier for the actors to put the right amount of energy in it (rather than sitting around a table), and this allows everyone watching to have a clearer idea of what the pantomime will be like; it allows the writer to hear the play aloud, and already start to hear which bits are in need of attention; it helps everyone in the room to get a clear idea immediately of who is playing which character; wardrobe departments can already get rough timings for quick costume changes. Above all it gives the production a running start, which can be wonderfully hectic fun, and can be a great way of your company bonding and relaxing into the rest of the rehearsal process.

Designer's presentation

For the designer it is a chance to share the set and costume designs in a presentation with the performers. Unlike the director, the designer may not have met them before. So it is important that the designs are presented clearly and sensitively. It is important to describe in detail the aspects of the set and costume that the company are going to interact with most. It will be difficult for them to take on board everything at this initial presentation. So put the design drawings, ground plan and photographic storyboard up on the walls of the rehearsal room; it will be beneficial for them to revisit these aspects when they get to that point in their rehearsals.

With the costumes it is important that the performers and choreographer get the opportunity to ask questions about how they will be able to move in them and where there are opportunities for visual gags from their look or the way that they might move with the body. It can also raise the possibility of requesting certain aspects of their clothing to be in rehearsals as soon as possible, which may help the actors get into their character. For example with skin parts it is crucial that heads and tails (even rehearsal substitutes) are worn by the performers at the earliest possible time, so that they can get accustomed to and play with what

Daisy the Cow was designed so that the body finished high enough to allow full movement of the legs as she frequently needed to dance (actors: Peter Holdway, and inside Daisy, Martine Burt and Alice Jackson).

these features will do. With false heads it can restrict hearing so it is important that they know this early. With characters such as the cow in *Jack and the Beanstalk* the full outfit should be in rehearsals from day one to allow the performers to understand how much dancing and movement it can do, and how long they can stay in the suit without overheating. In our version of Jack and the Beanstalk the cow needed to tap-dance so it was important to find out how to make sure that the hooves fitted over tap shoes and how we might mic the hooves to amplify the tap sounds.

REHEARSALS

The rehearsal period for a pantomime (as previously mentioned) can often be shorter than for a regular straight drama, and massively shorter than a musical, despite the fact that it can have enough songs and routines to put it into the 'musical' category.

So, rehearsals need to be structured and well-prepared. With a two-week rehearsal period with the company you ought to be able to do a very rough run of the whole pantomime by the end of the first week. It is good to let your cast know your plans as soon as possible. Some will want to learn the script in advance; others will want to learn the songs or have the music. Some won't be able to do any work in advance, but if they know what scenes will be run when, then they can organize what bits of script to learn for when, and therefore be as prepared as possible.

Assistant director

A good assistant director is worth their weight in gold. They can run scenes after the director has established the basic blocking. They can run lines with actors, rehearse with the junior chorus, run pre-rehearsed scenes, and if appropriate there may be a section or scene of the pantomime that they can direct in its entirety. A good assistant can help make the most of a short rehearsal period and give the actors more rehearsal time. This way an aspiring director can get a chance to work on a large production where their input can really make a difference.

Happening all over the place

When rehearsing at Watford Palace Theatre we would be doing the major scenes in the rehearsal room. The largest dressing room would have a keyboard set up in it and the musical director would work on the solos and duets in there. The first floor bar area would often be used to rehearse small scenes. The assistant director would be working with a couple of actors in the upper foyer, and other actors could be found running lines in most of the corridors. In fact the whole building was taken up with the pantomime's rehearsals!

Assistant designer

An assistant designer can be incredibly useful during the rehearsal process as all the departments are working flat-out and quite often want contact and approval/discussion with the designer at the same time. So to be able to delegate some of these jobs to an assistant can avoid holding up the progress. Also, it can quite often be useful for the designer to get a second opinion on some of the more important decisions and changes.

Certain parts of the design can also be delegated and this then allows them to work on and follow these items right through to the production without having to constantly check back with the designer. For example in *Jack and the Beanstalk* I had an assistant designer (Simon Wells), who took the idea of the cloud chair from my initial sketch, and modelled it, did the working drawings and followed it right through the workshop and onto the set.

Rehearsal day

Below is an example of a typical rehearsal day, when working with a large main cast and junior chorus. It is structured to achieve as much rehearsal happening simultaneously as possible, though it requires different rehearsal spaces. As you can see, in the mornings rehearsals can be very fragmented – some cast will be working on specific scenes with the director (or the assistant director), some with the choreographer, and the musical director will be working with individuals on solos and duets. At the end of the morning, the director will have rehearsed several scenes, as well as having looked in on the end of the various dancing/singing sessions. In the afternoon, the company pulls together more and the larger scenes are tackled.

The director's role in rehearsals

A director needs to have very clear goals for each day. Entrances and exits need to be worked out in advance, bearing in mind costume and set

	DIRECTOR	MUSICAL DIRECTOR	CHOREOGRAPHER	ASSISTANT DIRECTOR
10.00	Scene 2	Look at baddie's solo	Look at Dame's and Comic's dance	Look at lines for scene 3
10.45	Scene 3	Look at Dame's and Comic's duet	Look at Jack and Jill's dance	Go back over Scene 2
11.15	All to look at Dame's and Comic's song and dance			
11.30	BREAK			
11.45	Scene 4	Look at Jack and Jill's duet and dance	Go over Scene 3	
12.15	Scene 5	Jill's Solo	Baddie's dance	Go over Scene 4
12.45	Recap Jill and Jack's duet and dance, and baddie's dance/solo			
LUNCH				
2.00	Cast work with musical director, director and choreographer on the big opening number, and beginning Act 2 song.			
3.45	BREAK			
4.00	Junior chorus arrives and the whole company looks at opening scene.			
5.00	Most of the adult company are released, leaving Jack, baddie and sidekick who rehearse scenes 3 and 4 with the young people.			
5.45	BREAK. Adult company are released.			
6.00	Work with the young company on Act 2 opening dance.			
7.00	End call.			

changes. It is also good to have a rough idea of how you might want to block the scene, even if this idea changes in the rehearsal room. After all, a director will have been 'directing the scene' when talking through the set design with the designer many months previously.

An 'organic' approach to directing, where the decisions happen gradually in the rehearsal room (which can work so well for other forms of theatre), can take up time that is just not available. This may sound restrictive, but actually by making many of the practical, pragmatic decisions in advance, you can concentrate in rehearsals on character, story-telling and making the production as funny as possible!

By sticking to a timed plan, whilst you may initially have to skim over scenes that aren't working (when ideally you would want to keep rehearsing them till they are right), you and the company get a rough overview of the whole show. You can then go back and rehearse the parts that are working less well. How much you achieve will vary from day to day, but without a plan of how and when to cover all the scenes, you may find

yourself coming towards the end of the rehearsal period with a brilliant opening, and a very sketchy Act 2.

Build time in towards the end of the rehearsal period for at least two full run-throughs, preferably with one scheduled to coincide with the availability of the junior chorus, and your technical team – including wardrobe (who need to know where and when the quick changes occur). The run with the junior chorus can be organized so that each young team takes turns to enact the chorus roles in the piece, and when not performing become the actors' very first audience. This can be a huge boost to morale for all concerned.

Rehearsing 'business'

'Business' is the term for a section of the pantomime, which is normally humorous, non-verbal, and may require props or particular comic timing to get right. It might be a pie-fight, or a section where the comic character walks around with a large plank and others have to avoid it, etc. These need to end up looking slick and effortless to your audience, but can take up enormous amounts

Rehearsing part of the ballroom scene from Cinderella *using rehearsal handbags (actors: Kieran Buckeridge, Dale Superville and Debra Michaels) at Watford Palace Theatre.*

of time to rehearse – depending on how experienced your performers are, and how complicated the moment is. You need to allow regular rehearsal time throughout the process for these moments to be rehearsed: one rehearsal is needed to establish the blocking moves and timing; and subsequent shorter rehearsals are needed to perfect and practise the stunt.

Rehearsal props and costume

Due to the short rehearsal time, it is often crucial for props, or specific bits of costume (even if in prototype form) to be present early in rehearsals, otherwise precious time can be spent rehearsing something that doesn't work once the actual item appears. Baddies often need a cloak to rehearse with, and items such as hats or umbrellas may be needed for dance routines.

A prop for a gag or particular joke can be tried out in the early stages of rehearsal to see if the basic premise works, and then modifications and the final make can be done once this try-out has happened. If these items are made in isolation and only delivered late in rehearsals the prop may not fit with the action the actor has been doing, which can waste precious rehearsal time or result in that prop or moment being cut from the show.

CREATIVE CHANGES IN THE REHEARSAL PROCESS

It is so important to use the rehearsal process to test out aspects of the design and the script. This would seem an obvious statement, but with pantomime the lead-in time once in the theatre is usually very limited, and will offer little or no time for creative changes other than cutting something from the show.

Making cuts

It is crucial for the creative team to be as objective as possible during the rehearsals and technical week. At times certain dialogue/gags that have been instrumental to the development of the story or favourite bits of business or staging may need to

be cut from the show. Where this involves costumes, set or props then this should be ascertained as soon as possible to avoid wasting valuable making time. This might mean doing some of the scenes that are questionable out of order, or working quickly through the whole script to check for these situations. Quite often cuts are made because they are slowing down the pace or that they are superfluous to the telling of the story when the show is running too long.

For design it is important to keep very close contact with the director and the rehearsals to know when these changes might be occurring and to be able to offer up solutions or respond to requests at very short notice. There will be times when there is not enough time to make major changes, particularly in the case of the set. Then the designer has to be honest, and with the help of the production manager, set a cut-off point when

Jeff Nicholson as Alderman Fitzwarren doing his juggling with the shop's produce as part of a musical number (the items of fruit had to be made to a standard size to make them easier to juggle with).

everything has to be decided by, and if necessary be prepared to make cuts when time runs out.

Creative solutions

Where issues have been raised early enough in the rehearsals, and there are changes that will make existing items either function better or become

---

Boating troubles

In *Dick Whittington and his Cat*, the baddies were originally scripted to come on in a rowing boat and plant a bomb on the side of the *Saucy Sally* ship. In rehearsals it was ascertained that the rowing boat would not be as manoeuvrable as required and would block too much of the side of the boat from the audience perspective in the stalls. So the idea of a rubber dinghy was suggested. This was then quickly designed around a small inflatable dinghy and fastened to a wooden base with disc castors mounted underneath, with the idea of moving and steering it with the use of oars.

However, when this had been built it did not work as hoped, and went through several changes. Finally, the dinghy was mounted on more robust and multi-directional wheels and a skirt added under the lip of the dinghy to hide them. This enabled holes to be cut in the base so that the character at the back could use their feet as well as an oar to manoeuvre the dinghy into the positions required. It was important to get this right to maintain the pace of the scene and provide the audience with the best possible view of the action.

King Rat and Nat the Rat in their rat dinghy, having just planted a bomb on the side of the ship (actors: Peter Holdway and Natasha Cox, with Dale Superville, Tom Bradley, Sia Kiwa, Liza Pulman and Howard Coggins).

funnier, then creative improvements can and should be made.

It is important for the writer, director and designer to keep looking out for the moments that can lift an aspect of a scene and either enhance or create a new gag. Also once the actors get to play in the rehearsals they can quite often come up with new props that will support or punctuate the 'business' they are creating. Some performers have talents that can be incorporated into the pantomime, and these may only come to light during the rehearsals, such as juggling, theatrical routines or certain dance moves. These could be good opportunities for extra business but might require extra props or costume adaptations.

Costume fittings

Even with a very short rehearsal period there will need to be fittings for the costumes. This will always be kept to a minimum and in most cases can be sorted within the rehearsal schedule. Most characters will need only one fitting. However, the actor requiring the most time is of course the dame, because of the numerous outfits.

Fittings are a good opportunity for the designer and the wardrobe staff to discuss any quick change

concerns or specific needs that have not been recorded on the rehearsal notes. Some fittings might need to be ad hoc, with costumes being brought into the rehearsal room to be tried on during appropriate breaks. A photographic record of all fittings should be done to show the director, as it is unlikely that they will be able to attend; furthermore, on occasions even the designer may be absent due to other commitments.

Slosh scenes

Firstly, a check for allergies must be done with all the actors who come in to contact with any gunk/cream/dough (as previously mentioned), because with performances often twice daily for several weeks any reaction or discomfort will increase with repetition. Often the consistency of dough, gloop or pie-cream needs to be tested. Some

Fitting with Peter Shorey for Widow Twankey in Aladdin, using a cardboard box as a pattern to ascertain the correct size for the washing machine skirt on the laundry outfit (with costume maker, Dawn Evans, and head of wardrobe, Kirsty Rowe).

The cream pie had to be edible so that Tommy the Cat could lap it off his face (Dale Superville in Dick Whittington and his Cat).

of this testing can be done by the stage management department in isolation, but there needs to be special time set aside in rehearsal for doing the slosh scene fully.

In the slosh run provision should be made for covering up the rehearsal room floor, and overalls and shower facilities at the ready for the actors concerned. It is good to try this around the middle of the rehearsal period, once the scene has been blocked, and initially rehearsed. This 'run' will ascertain if any moves need to be changed to make the scene work more effectively or alterations to the consistency or look of the slosh to make it stick or flow better. Once the 'mess' created by the scene has been discovered, decisions about cleaning up can be finalized, as this might need cloths, buckets and mops pre-set within a scene.

The added bonus of trying these scenes out in rehearsals is that you get some lovely rehearsal photos to help your publicity!

Sound

If you have a lot of live music in your production and the cast are going to be wearing microphones, it is a very good idea to have your sound designer and/or operator attending a couple of rehearsal runs – preferably with their sound equipment and the microphones. A pantomime can be a very complicated show to operate and the more practice they get in advance, the easier your technical rehearsal will be.

Cueing meeting

Again, due to the complexity of a pantomime, it can be a good idea to have a full cueing meeting prior to the technical rehearsal. Your deputy stage manager (DSM) will have hopefully been making copious notes during rehearsals, and asking questions about where to put particular cues, but it is best to have dedicated time to sit down and get the cues in the book together. Some lighting designers work out their own cues from watching a couple of run-throughs, and then have a meeting with the director and DSM during the plotting sessions.

TECHNICAL REHEARSALS

Technical rehearsals are the rehearsals that take place onstage with full set, costume, lighting and sound, running through the show for all the technical staff to practise scene changes etc., and for the creative team to make sure that all is working and looking as expected. Again, because there is so much to do in a relatively short time, good planning is essential. The production itself needs to be in good shape – that is, the actors should have had at least a couple of full run-throughs prior to running the show in the technical rehearsal. Certain things about the technical rehearsals may be different for pantomime than for other shows:

- Band call: a specific rehearsal for the musicians who will play live music, if they haven't been involved in rehearsals. This can also give the sound designer and engineer a chance to check their levels for each of the songs.
- Sitzprobe: a section of the technical devoted to checking the sound levels etc. of your cast and their microphones by running through all the musical numbers.
- Lighting: the plotting session for pantomime can take much longer than for other types of production. Always consult the lighting designer about this, to make sure there is enough time.
- Junior chorus: to limit the time the young chorus are kept hanging around, try 'teching' the chorus sections first (on the Saturday before the start of technical week). This will speed things up, and ensure that you are not keeping young people away from school unnecessarily, or up too late on a school night. Also, as their scenes tend to crop up sporadically throughout the show, it gives the stage team a chance to look at most scenes briefly – a kind of dry run, before the technical rehearsals start in earnest.
- Sing-through: because a great deal of the lighting and sound cues happen during the songs, it can be good to start your technical rehearsal with a sing-through. It can warm the

actors up and give the technical departments at least one go at each 'number' before having to approach them in the full tech.

For the main technical rehearsal there is a temptation to do a cue-to-cue style rehearsal, but it is best to do every part of every scene. In this way you should be able to spot every potential difficulty and find a solution within the next day or so. By skimming through you may overlook a problem, which is much more difficult to rectify once the production is up and running.

The technical rehearsal for such a large production can be a fraught time, but the director must endeavour to keep a sense of calm, and as much fun as possible. It can feel wonderful to see all the ideas that you've been having for nearly a year finally coming together on stage. Keep remembering this and pass on the feeling to the cast and crew – they will be feeling anxious and tired, and any words of praise and enthusiasm will be much appreciated.

Understanding the time constraints

The set and costume are often not completely ready at the beginning of the technical rehearsals; this is due to the amount of work required with a pantomime and the tight schedule. It is usual that early mornings are the onstage time for completing the scenic items and set dressing. Here they can have dedicated time and not delay the rehearsals for the band and actors. It is, however, important that all the functioning aspects of the set that the actors interact with are complete, so that they get a chance to work with these in the tech right from the beginning.

In *Cinderella* the hands of the clock were not rigged and working till the day of the first previews. This was later than anyone would have liked but because it was something that was attached to the backcloth and not something that the actors connected with, it was continually pushed down the list of priorities. It is funny to think that we were close to doing our first preview without the clock being able to show it was midnight – a fairly important narrative moment in the story of *Cinderella*.

Onstage chat with the actors, whilst lighting is being plotted (director Joyce Branagh with actors Andrew Bolton and Allyson Brown). Note that as this is an early technical rehearsal, there are still scenic elements to be completed (lighting design by John Harris).

PREVIEWS

These are a great test of what is working and not working. The director will be looking for all the moments on stage that are working well or needing some tweaks – deciding what notes to give, and so on. But it is also good to watch the audience, and listen to their reactions. As has already been said, a young audience will get bored and shuffle around in the bits that they are not interested in. Note carefully where these sections are; if they happen in two consecutive previews there is definitely a problem. Perhaps it's a song that goes on too long, a section of dialogue that is flagging and needs to be cut or spoken with more pace and

'Adults' standing in for the children onstage for the songsheet (Dale Superville with Central School of Speech and Drama student Jaemi Bermudez).

urgency, or a scene change that is taking too long.

It can also be really useful to have an invited 'adult 'audience in for the final dress rehearsal as this can really help the actors prepare for the evening performances when there are more families than school parties. The junior chorus can be a good barometer of certain aspects of the show but to get to understand the more adult references having a local group or college come in can be ideal. Also, it can be great fun and a challenge for the actor/actors when you get 'adults' up onstage to do the songsheet.

If it is at all possible after the first couple of previews (often a Saturday matinée and evening), try to build some time off into the schedule – even if it is just a day. Secondly, consider including an extra day of rehearsals. The company may feel that this 'extra rehearsal' is precious time that they could spend relaxing after a hectic week, but as a writer or director, this is your last chance to cut sections that aren't working, tighten, or re-rehearse sections that need it, and reassure people about sections that they may still feel unsure about. Without this extra day, there is virtually no point to previews – they show you what is not working, but give you no opportunity to change things.

Whatever the problems that crop up during a preview, a good meeting with the creative team can often offer up suggestions that can be put into place on the extra rehearsal day. This will then ensure that your production is the tightest and most entertaining it can be, and that the pantomime you have all created is absolutely ready to face the general public and the critics.

WATFORD PALACE THEATRE
CENTENARY
WITH DALE SUPERVILLE RETURNING AS THE CAT!
DICK WHITTINGTON & HIS CAT
Written and Directed by Joyce Branagh
Designed by Keith Orton

12 PROMOTION AND FUTURE PLANNING

As a conclusion to this book it useful to look at some useful ways to promote your current pantomime and consider how to plan for future productions.

THE EARLY BIRD ...

However you approach the promotion of your pantomime, do it early. Unlike any other kind of performance, audiences for pantomime often book their tickets a long way in advance, and so you want to make sure that when they are choosing which production to book, your show is already being advertised, and if possible, that tickets are available to buy.

Some theatres announce their next year's pantomime (and put it on sale) during their current show. This can create a buzz about both shows simultaneously. Often next year's pantomime is advertised in the programme, or leaflets are handed out to the audience as they leave announcing that tickets are on sale for next year's production, normally at a discounted rate.

Schools and family groups may have favourite dates that they like to attend, so if you offer them the opportunity to book early, they may walk straight from their seats to the box-office window, or ring or go online and book tickets the following day!

By doing this, many theatres are able to accrue a substantial amount in early ticket sales, providing a basis of the production budget for the following year's show.

DECIDING ON THE NEXT PANTOMIME

If putting the above strategy into operation, you will have to plan well in advance, and know which title you intend to stage next. If you are tackling your first pantomime, but intend this to be an annual event for your company, then you may want to think ahead for a few years, and make your choices accordingly (*see* Chapter 2 for the different titles and their audience appeal.)

You may have a particular anniversary or event that you wish to commemorate, which may

OPPOSITE: *Peter Holdway as King Rat and Dale Superville as Tommy Cat on a publicity event for* Dick Whittington and his Cat *outside Watford Palace Theatre.*

influence your choice of pantomime. At Watford Palace we knew that the theatre had its centenary in 2008, and we felt that the story of *Dick Whittington* would give us the best basis for a pantomime set in 1908. So, from 2005 the theatre was choosing the intervening pantomime titles with that event in mind. The final script for *Dick Whittington* had historical references, was very firmly set in Watford, and exuded a celebratory feel.

Some theatres will have a policy of doing just the five or six most popular pantomime titles and keep rotating them in order, working on the principle that by the time it comes around again the young audience that saw it previously will now have grown out of being taken to the pantomime, or will find different aspects of the show appealing and appreciate the story on a different level. With this policy there is also the possibility (providing that there is space) to store certain crucial and expensive elements of the staging and re-work/re-use them when it comes around again. This can work for such things as the flying carpet, Cinderella's carriage, or the beanstalk. You might even advertise these for hire and make some money from them in the years when they are not being used. If your preference is for using new or different scripts each time, you can adopt a new approach to writing the same basic story the next time you do it.

Other theatres will choose to intersperse the most popular ones with the pantomimes that are not so immediately recognizable. For example a sequence such as:

Cinderella
Puss in Boots
Aladdin
Sleeping Beauty
Jack and the Beanstalk
Mother Goose
Dick Whittington
Robinson Crusoe
Snow White and the Seven Dwarfs

This broadens the repertoire and the supposedly less popular ones get supported (both financially, and from repeat bookings) by having a more popular one the year before.

METHODS OF PROMOTION

'Branding'

Most marketing professionals feel that it is good to have one picture that is used to 'brand' a production. In this way, a certain image or lettering style is intrinsically linked to your production throughout its development and subsequent advertising, such as posters, leaflets, website, and newspapers. If starting your advertising early, this image might be created before the script and design, so it should be something that is appealing but generic to the title. Consider the specific audience that you are aiming at. If you want to attract a family audience, make sure the design of the pantomime publicity material is not so young that it appears your show is only for small children, and not too sophisticated to put off the younger members of the family.

Think very hard about the lettering style – the 'title treatment'. This should be able to stand alone, because in some press coverage there may not be room to include the full graphic. The title treatment must be carefully chosen to specifically link to your pantomime.

A hand-drawn or quirky typeface works better than selecting an established one as you can give it a cartoon, storybook or fairy-tale quality that has a bit of pantomime magic. Think about your potential audience and what will attract them, and think about whether it ties in to the style of the actual production. If it is a traditional family pantomime your publicity material needs to reflect that. Taking an approach that is too photographic and contemporary may deter many purchasers.

Local publicity

When you are trying to promote the production in the media, keep most of your ideas linked to the locality of the theatre. Most people go to a pantomime near them. This doesn't mean you can't create a buzz and get people coming from

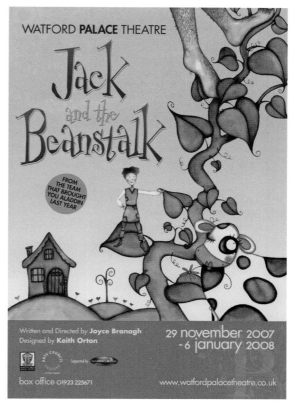

The programme cover from Cinderella; *publicity flyer for* Jack and the Beanstalk.

further away, but the majority of your audience will live within a few miles of the theatre, so keep that in mind with all promotional activity.

Getting your image around

This will be very much dictated by your budget, but you will want to try and get your pantomime image around and about your local area.

Billboards, posters and leaflets

If affordable, billboards in a busy place can be a great way to make sure everyone knows about your production. If the town has a main train station or bus terminus or busy bus stops, then these can be great places where people spend time waiting or passing through. Some companies get banners made and stretch them across the main

road of the town. With all these ideas, you will need to check with your local council about applying for permission. Decide upon the best time to put up your billboards; because people book pantomime early, you may want to think about posting them in September/October rather than just before the production.

Get as many local businesses and shops as possible to display your poster in their windows. Similarly with leaflets, local distribution is essential, and the earlier the better. You may want to try and organize a day towards the end of school holidays or autumn half-term where you have a leafleting session in the town. Getting people into costume to hand out the leaflets can be fun, and attract a lot more attention. In some town centres you will need official permission to do this.

Howard Coggins as Sarah the Cook serving at John Lewis in Watford, a photograph opportunity for the press and also a means of promoting the pantomime to the local community.

Local press

A good eye-catching image will be well worth the cost of advertising. Towards Christmas, some papers and magazines have a specific Christmas entertainment listings section.

There may be a possibility for additional coverage in your local paper by 'drip feeding' them different 'news' stories to do with the production in the months approaching the show. These include announcing the pantomime itself, the auditions for the junior chorus, a competition, or perhaps a need for a specific prop. Think of ideas that will catch the eye or the imagination, and if possible provide a great photo to go with it. It is worth trying to find a series of interesting facts and figures, or associations with current news stories, that can get coverage and keep the interest in the production fresh and ongoing.

A good way of getting coverage can be to get involved with local events that might be taking place just prior to the opening of the pantomime, such as the switching on of the Christmas lights in the town. Another could involve the company visiting a local charity, school, hospital, or retirement home to entertain or bring some Christmas joy to proceedings.

Advertising can be made easier if you have a celebrity or TV actor in the production, but even if not it is good to look for possible interest areas, such as an actor returning to their home town, or a popular actor returning for another season. You could also advertise your twist on the retelling of the pantomime story, but be careful not to give too much of the 'game' away and spoil the surprise for the audiences that come.

Local radio

This can be a great way of getting your pantomime advertised. If you can approach your local radio station early enough, they might be interested in working together to create advertisements, competitions and interviews which can help promote the production. In return they may want their logo displayed on your publicity material.

Photos

It is good to set up a photo-shoot at least three months in advance of the show (earlier if you can), as this can be a way of the theatre announcing their Autumn season alongside a first look at who is in the show. Because this takes place so far ahead it is unlikely that actual costumes for the actors will be ready. However, it is worth the cost of hiring some, as costumed characters will have much

One of the press publicity photographs for Cinderella, *featuring the Ugly Sisters (Dale Superville and Kieran Buckeridge) and Cinderella (Allyson Brown) using hired costumes from York Theatre Royal.*

more impact. For the dame, it is better to hire a costume rather than show one of the spectacular frocks from the coming production and give too much away.

Sponsorship

Local businesses may be willing to sponsor the production financially in exchange for logos etc. on your publicity material, or for advertising in the programme. They may also offer you in-kind support; for example, a local shopping centre might allow a permanent stand in the main foyer area, encourage promotional activity near their 'Santa's grotto', or perhaps allow a short performance of a song. Bookshops and toy shops may encourage visits from actors in costume, and the local council may give more publicity and exposure to your production in exchange for an organized workshop or a reading at a local library.

Website, Facebook and Twitter

If at all possible you need to have a presence on the web, and a website for the company is pretty much essential. Here you can not only let your potential audience know what is on and where, but also give them an indication of the sort of production it will

be, and encourage them to book early.

Many productions now 'blog' to let their audience know what is going on in the run-up to a production. This can provide on-the-spot news from the rehearsal room, as well as showing rehearsal photos and sneak peeks of set and costume.

Audiences love to know what it is like 'behind the scenes' and so social sites such as Facebook and Twitter can be a useful way of communicating with friends of the theatre, from the writing and design period right through rehearsals and into the production weeks. The communication can work both ways, so not only can the company update people on what they are getting up to, but also it is a great chance for feedback on attendance and what they enjoyed when they came to see the show. Critics' reviews can be useful, but there is nothing better than getting feedback from your paying public.

Video trailers

Many websites now sport video trailers which visitors to the website can easily access to get a further insight into the production. These might be as simple as an interview with the director or a

The programme from Jack and the Beanstalk *showing activities for children.*

couple of the actors, or may be a mini-film in itself. Often these can be done relatively economically, and young film-makers are often keen to offer their services.

Programmes

It is really important to create an interesting and accurate programme. An interesting programme can offer not only the necessary show information but also include interesting pantomime facts, games and puzzles for the children. This can be something that they do partly whilst in the theatre but can also have things to complete once they leave, e.g. a colouring-in page that then can form a competition, with prizes of tickets for the family for next year's show.

It must be accurate and give thanks to the people who may have been instrumental in getting the show on and/or have given their time for free (a name in the programme might be their only reward). Plus, it is important to make a fuss of the children that form your junior chorus, as their parents and grandparents want to see their pictures and names in print.

Kerb appeal

It can be really effective to make sure that the minute the audiences approach the theatre you are welcoming them into the world of pantomime.

Use coloured lights (or even moving light) to illuminate the facade of the theatre. This will immediately change the appearance and add to the expectation of a good night out. This use of the outside can be taken further by adding objects or banners that help promote the particular pantomime story. For example, having a giant hand or foot coming out of a wall or window, or perhaps the tendrils of the beanstalk climbing up the wall can make a witty statement and add to the interest for passers-by, creating kerb appeal.

Your foyer area

Once inside the theatre, spend time dressing the front-of-house areas to carry on the themes of the show. The youngsters will love it when they are surrounded by bits of the story that they are about to see.

You can also include in this your merchandise stand, selling assorted wands, swords and flashing bunny ears. Some of these items can have very tenuous links with the subject matter of the panto, but they appeal to children (big and small) and help them feel part of the evening's fun. They will also give them something to play with whilst waiting for the show to commence. There is a wide range of this sort of merchandising that can be bought in to sell on, and it can be a good way of bringing in extra revenue. It can be quite overpowering and even a little distracting at busy children's matinées seeing the whole auditorium light up with a kaleidoscope of these flashing toys. However, they can be of help when the show goes to blackout, as it might be a distraction for young children to make them less frightened by the dark.

Don't forget you need an audience

Whatever you do in the way of publicizing and promoting your pantomime, remember to spend time planning and making this part as effective and as thoroughly considered as the rest of the show. It is no good spending hours and hours creating the most beautiful production if you don't get enough people through the doors to make it a success and bring in enough money to do another one next year!

TIME TO REFLECT

When getting to the end of the process and saying goodbye to the creative team and the cast it is good to step back and appreciate all that has happened. It is worth making a few notes about the things that really worked, as well as the things that you might want to rethink, before they get forgotten in the mists of time. Where were the weaknesses in the story and where did it get everyone really excited? What is really enthusing you about doing it all again?

One of the great things about being a writer, director or designer is the level of anonymity that you have when mingling with the audience in the bar after the show. It can be good to eavesdrop on those conversations that are analyzing the show

The company of Dick Whittington and his Cat *waving goodbye at the end of the finale (lighting by John Harris).*

without having to ask that direct question, 'Well what did you think?'

There is one lasting memory from *Cinderella*, our first production at Watford Palace Theatre. Two little brothers were heard discussing the show during the interval after Cinderella's transformation. One turned to the other and said:

'How did Cinderella change her dress so quickly?'
'Don't you know?'
'No. How did it happen?'
'You silly. It was magic.'

GLOSSARY

backcloth: a stretched cloth, the furthest upstage, attached to a flying bar and spanning the width of the stage. Fixed to the floor, or, containing a sleeve that houses a piece of metal conduit to weight the bottom edge down; often has a painted scene covering its entire surface.

bleed-through: when the lighting of a scene switches from in front of a gauze to behind it, illuminating the scene behind the gauze.

built-in practicals: the lights that are designed and built into items of scenery.

cross-fade: where instead of a sudden snap from one lighting state to the next, the states overlap and create a seamless change.

crossover: the means by which actors and crew can cross behind the set during the performance, either behind the back wall of the set or via a theatre corridor.

cut-cloths: are painted scenic cloths that have cut-away sections such as doorways or have detailed cut-away edges on such things as overhanging foliage. Netting is sometimes used to help support the cut-out sections.

dramaturg: in Britain this role is often very similar to that of a script editor, a person who works alongside the writer to develop the script, making suggestions on character, structure and style. It can also refer to someone who researches into historical and social backgrounds to assist a playwright, director and/or design team with the development of a production.

flattage: flat scenic structures; either wood-covered frames, or canvas-covered frames that are arranged within a set as vertical walling.

fly-tower: the section of a theatre, above the acting area, where the flown items of scenery are stored when not on stage.

French braced flats: the type of scenic flat that has a triangular hinged support that is attached to the back, which when opened out and weighted will be self standing.

frontcloth: a flown downstage cloth that is designed to either create an image for an audience to view before the production starts, or, a means of covering a scene change upstage of the cloth.

gobo: a metal cut-out, located in front of a lamp to project a shaped silhouette onto the stage, such as a window, leaves, etc.

grave trap: a section of the stage floor that has a built in trap-door mechanism to allow it to be lowered for items of set or props to be loaded on, and then raised up to stage level.

ground rows: a low horizontal strip of scenery (possibly cut-out) that stretches across the width of stage and disguises the join between the back cloth or cyclorama and the stage floor, as well as adding upstage perspective.

header: a section of soft or hard masking that is suspended across the width of the stage to help mask/conceal the lighting and flying rig.

lining in: the process of adding the black or

coloured outlines to add definition to painted cloths.

open stage: is the first aspect of the design (for a pantomime), that includes the floor and the portals that create the framing for the rest of the design.

Plastazote: is a compressed polyethylene foam that can be cut, moulded and glued together to create structures for costume or props.

portal: are the vertical set pieces, (like side flats) that frame the space and the design, and help mask the wings. They are arranged horizontally across the stage usually diminishing in aperture size the further upstage they go, creating a tunnel like effect.

proscenium: the open-framed wall that divides the acting area from the auditorium.

pyro pod: is the box that houses the pyrotechnic charges for onstage special effects.

returns: sections of flattage that are added at right-angles to legs on either side of stage that give depth or help mask the stage.

shark's-tooth gauze: a form of scenic gauze used as painted cloths, which, due to its structured mesh, can become transparent when lit from behind.

sightlines: from the ends of seating rows; the extreme viewpoints from which the audience can see the set and into the wings. These viewpoints should include the stalls, circle and balcony where appropriate.

Sitsprobe: where the singers and the band work together for the first time on stage. This is normally a still rehearsal, and concentrates on the quality of the sound, the acoustics, microphones, amplification, and the mix of the music in the auditorium and on stage.

sliders: are scenic flats suspended on tracks that run horizontally across the stage. They can be manually operated or moved via a pulley system fed into the offstage wings.

slosh scene: A comic scene where the action involves getting messy, with the actors getting covered in a variety of different types of gunge or water. These are commonly cooking, make-up or decorating scenes.

star cloth: is a black full-stage cloth that has lighting in series stitched into the cloth to create a star-lit sky.

tormentors: are the entrances that allow the performers to access downstage of the frontcloth. These are of particular importance for the spirits of good and evil to use. Remembering that Good enters stage right, and Evil enters stage left.

treads: are the theatrical term for stairs.

ACKNOWLEDGEMENTS

It would have been impossible to have completed this book without the following people's contributions.

From the pantomimes at Watford Palace Theatre

Our fellow collaborators:
Writer of *Cinderella* and *Aladdin*: Joe Graham.
Lighting design: John Harris.
Choreography: Nikki Woollaston.
Sound design: Dave Glover.
Musical directors: Matt Smith, Stu Barker and Magnus Gilljam.
Musical supervisor and arranger: John Rigby.
Artistic directors who commissioned the productions: Brigid Larmour and Lawrence Till.

The actors whose great performances can be seen throughout this book:

Cinderella
Madeline Appiah, Andrew Bolton, Stephen Boswell, Allyson Brown, Kieran Buckeridge, Daniel Crowder, Debra Michaels, Gina Murray, Oliver Tompsett, and Dale Superville.
Junior chorus: Lauren Armstrong, Lewis Bingley, Alex Butcher, Ronald Chabvuka, Rose Chabvuka, Gabrielle Foley, William Hemsley, Luke Meredith, Lauren McDonnell, Brodie O'Shea, Chloe Robinson and Jessica Walker.

Aladdin
John Alastair, Nicola Blackman, Kieran Buckeridge, Stefan Butler, Howard Coggins, Rachel Grimshaw, Joanne Redman, Peter Shorey, Dale Superville and David Webber.
Junior chorus: Margaret Archibong, Hayley Baldwin, Lewis Bingley, Ross Calder, Serafina Conboy, Emily Deighton, Asher Ibeke Cole, Lauren McDonnell, Ama Opong, Brodie O'Shea, Chloe Sherman and Raymond Thompson.

Jack and the Beanstalk
Richard Ashton, Martine Burt, Ricardo Coke-Thomas, Natasha Cox, Peter Holdway, Alice Jackson, Tania Mathurin, Andrea Miller, Christopher Robert and Dale Superville.
Junior chorus: Vienna Best, Tomás Brennan, Serafina Conboy, Emily Dawes, Tom Emberton, Lauren McDonnell, Jack McDonnell, Niamh O'Brien, Ama Opong, Aurélie Sukhnandan, Hannah Thompson and Joshua Whitehead.

Dick Whittington and his Cat
Tom Bradley, Howard Coggins, Natasha Cox, Peter Holdway, Alice Jackson, Sia Kiwa, Jeff Nicholson, Liza Pulman and Dale Superville.
Junior chorus: Tomás Brennan, Serafina Conboy, James Conder, Kira Matthews, Jack McDonnell, Lauren McDonnell, Lindelani Moyo, Taylor O'Dwer, Tia Pereira-Grieves, Emily Sanderson, Aurélie Sukhnandan, Joshua Whitehead.

Assistant directors: Anthony Biggs, David Cottis, Katy Silverton, Hannah Pantin and Holly McBride.
Assistant designers: Mike Bell, Jeremy Walker, Maggie Bradley, and Simon Wells.
Production managers: Ali Fellows, Matthew Ledbury and Felix Davies.
Head of wardrobe: Kirsty Rowe, with Jocelyn Creighton and Jo Norton.
Additional costumes by John Brooking, Dawn Evans, Margaret Brownfoot, Tina Kennedy, Heather Rayat, Lorna Clayton, Katy Bradford, Sue Nicholson, Sarah Ferdinando, World of Fantasy, and York Theatre Royal.
Wigs by Felicite Gillham.
Scenery construction team: Dave Agnew and Tip

Pargeter (Heads of Construction), with James Weatherby, Heather Jenkins and Alan Gibbs.
Scenic artists: Sue Dunlop and Aimee Bunyard.
Prop makers: Graham Gilmour, June Douglas and Mike Bell.
Stage management team: James Oakley, Saira Baker and Sarah Rhodes-Canning.
Electrics: Richmond Rudd, Dave Starmer and Francis Johnstone.
Programme and leaflet graphics: Laura Irwin.
And all the other staff at Watford Palace Theatre past and present, who have contributed to the success of the productions.

Staff and Students from Central School of Speech and Drama who contributed to the productions or content within the book
Caroline Townsend, Nick Moran, Alastair Noonan and Jane Cowood.
Lucie Shilton, Rhys Tucker, Beth Morris, Christabel Cant, Caroline Shelley, Abi Emmett, Emma King-Marsh, Joe Vassallo, Carla Macaluso, Louisa Mozzilli, Katie Muldoon, Janice Gorringe, Sarah Kier, Vanessa Leadbitter, Lucy Schmidt, Charlotte Nicholls, Heather Dolan, Megan Hunt, Jade Peplar, Danielle Martin, James Hirst, Lisa Else and Hersilia Leorca.

Other theatres and pantomime producers who have contributed to the images and content of the book
Oldham Coliseum Theatre; Theatre Royal, Bury St Edmunds; York Theatre Royal; Stafford Gatehouse Theatre; First Family Entertainment; Qdos Entertainment.

Professionals who have given time and interviews to add to the content
Set and costume designers: Terry Parsons, Ian Westbrook, Will Hargreaves, Celia Perkins, Simon Wells and Philip Engleheart.
Lighting designers: John Harris, Nick Moran and Ben Cracknell.
Production: Ali Fellows and Alastair Noonan.
Musical director/composer: Zara Nunn.

Photographs
Most of the photographs are supplied by Keith Orton with further production photographs by:
Manuel Harlan (www.manuelharlan.co.uk)
Ian Tilton (www.iantilton.net/theatre)
Keith Mindham (www.keithmindham.com)
Dennis Gilbert (www.dennisgilbert.com)
Robert Day and Philip Engleheart.

Readers who have given feedback on writing
Arthur Orton, Alan Bagnall, Zara Nunn and Rebecca Hutchens.

Keith would like to personally thank his partner Mike Bell who not only has worked alongside him throughout the pantomimes as an assistant designer/prop maker, but also provided the support and cups of tea needed to keep going when writing this book. Also Sue Dunlop, a close friend and amazing scenic artist whose work he admires and whom he has been lucky enough to have had as a scenic artist on all of his pantomime designs.

Joyce would like personally to thank her husband, Andy Fraser, for putting up with all the talk of pantomime for the past decade.

FURTHER READING AND RESEARCH

BOOKS

Bicât, T. with Staines, R. and Winslow, C., *Pantomime* (The Crowood Press, 2004)

Harris, P. and Hudd, R., *The Pantomime Book – The Only Known Collection of Pantomime Jokes in Captivity* (Peter Owen, 2001)

Latham, P., *It's Behind You* (New Holland Publishers, 2004)

Moran, N., *Performance Lighting Design* (A&C Black, 2007)

Orton, K., *Model Making for the Stage* (Crowood Press, 2004)

Robbins, N., *Slapstick and Sausages: The Evolution of Pantomime* (Trapdoor Publications, 2002)

Taylor, M., *British Pantomime Performance* (Intellect Books, 2007)

Thorne, G., *Stage Design* (Crowood Press, 1999)

Thorne, G., *Technical Drawing for Stage Design* (Crowood Press, 2010)

Wilson, A. E., *King Panto – The Story of Pantomime* (Dutton, 1935)

When a particular pantomime story has been chosen, collect and read as many children's picture books on that theme as possible. This will give you a broader knowledge of how the story has already been interpreted and how they have been captured illustratively.

USEFUL WEBSITES

www.its-behind-you.com – for excellent up-to-date information, history, and outlines of different pantomime stories.

www.bigpantoguide.co.uk – listings of the pantomimes that are taking place nationwide.

www.thestage.co.uk – reviews pantomimes nationwide; can be a good opportunity to analyse current trends and most popular titles.

www.vam.ac.uk/collections/theatre_performances – the Theatre Museum as part of the Victoria and Albert Museum. A valuable resource of programmes, scripts and filmed productions.

INDEX